A QUESTION OF CONSENT

A QUESTION

Innocence and
Complicity in
The Glen Ridge
Rape Case

OF CONSENT

PETER
LAUFER

Mercury House

San Francisco

Photo of Superior Court Judge R. Benjamin Cohen (page xiv) and Alan Zegas (page xv) by Bill Kostroun, courtesy of the *New Jersey Law Journal*. Photos of Christopher Archer (page xi) and of the prosecutors (pages xiv and 42) courtesy of Wide World Photos, Inc. Photos of Thomas Ford Jr., Michael Querques, and Louis Esposito (page xiv) courtesy of New Jersey News Photos.

United States Constitution, First Amendment: Congress shall make no law respecting an establishment of religion, or prohibiting the free exercise thereof; or abridging the freedom of speech, or of the press; or the right of the people peaceably to assemble, and to petition the Government for a redress of grievances.

Page design and typesetting: Po Bronson

Mercury House and colophon are registered trademarks of
Mercury House, Incorporated
Printed on recycled, acid-free paper
Manufactured in the United States of America

Library of Congress Cataloging-in-Publication Data
Laufer, Peter
    A question of consent : innocence and complicity in the Glen Ridge rape case / Peter Laufer
        p. cm.
    ISBN 1-56279-059-5 (acid-free paper)
    1. Archer, Christopher—Trials, litigation, etc. 2. Scherzer, Kevin—Trials, litigation, etc. 3. Scherzer, Kyle—Trials, litigation, etc. 4. Trials (Rape)—New Jersey—Newark. 5. Gang rape—New Jersey—Glen Ridge. 6. Mentally handicapped women—Crimes against—New Jersey—Glen Ridge. I. Title.
KF224.A73L38 1994
345.73'02523—dc20
[347.3052523]   93-42464
                                                                          CIP

5   4   3   2   1

Again, with love to

Sheila

for the teachings

The injury to personal integrity involved in forced sex is the reason that forced sex should be considered a serious crime even where there is no weapon or beating. Whether one adheres to the "rape as sex" school or the "rape as violence" school, the fact remains that what makes rape different from other crimes is that rape is a sexual violation—a violation of the most personal, most intimate, and most offensive kind.

—Susan Estrich, rape victim, social critic, and law professor

Sex is a turbulent power that we are not in control of; it is a dark force. The sexes are at war with each other. That's part of the excitement and interest of sex. It's the dark realm of the night. When you enter the realm of the night, horrible things can happen there.

—Camille Paglia, social critic and humanities professor

Boys will be boys. Pranksters. Fool-arounds. Do crazy things. Experiment with life and disregard their parents. Boys will be boys.

—Michael Querques, lawyer for one of the Glen Ridge rapists

Rape is torture.

—Amnesty International policy statement

Contents

Principal
Figures

THE VICTIM:
"Betty Harris," adopted as an infant in 1972 by her Glen Ridge parents, already diagnosed as mentally handicapped—a diagnosis initially and erroneously identified as correctable. "She was always in the very slow range," says her mother.

THE CONVICTED RAPISTS:
Christopher Archer, identified by the prosecution as the "mastermind" behind the crime.

Kevin and Kyle Scherzer, the twins whose basement is used as the venue for the crime. "You can't put a price tag on fun!" is the way Kyle sums up his philosophy in his high school yearbook.

Bryant Grober, who, after Betty performs fellatio on him, slinks off to a corner and is convicted only of conspiracy. His senior class yearbook quote is, "If you're walking on thin ice, you might as well dance."

CO-CONSPIRATORS WHO PLEAD GUILTY:
Peter Quigley, who pleads guilty on April 14, 1992, to endangering the welfare of an incompetent person, a relatively minor crime in

New Jersey, called a "disorderly persons offense." He agrees to testify if called as a witness and waives his Fifth Amendment rights.

Paul Archer, who pleads guilty to the same crime acknowledged by Quigley. Archer's false testimony proves to be a disaster for his brother and the other rapists. An insight into his character is offered by the prosecutors when they reveal the results of community service work he was sentenced to perform after an arrest for public drunkenness. Assigned to mail renewal license forms to dog owners, Archer adorned the forms with obscenities.

TEAMMATES INITIALLY INDICTED WHO DID NOT STAND TRIAL:
(Charges dropped at the request of Betty's parents)
John Maher is charged with joining in the conspiracy to lure Betty Harris to the basement, but not with sexual assault.

Richard Corcoran, Jr., son of a Glen Ridge policeman, is identified by prosecutors as having made incriminating statements about the Scherzers, Archer, and Grober. As a result, his case is severed from the others. "Is that the light I see at the end of the tunnel," his yearbook quote haunts him, "or is it just another train coming?"

ESSEX COUNTY ASSISTANT PROSECUTORS:
Elizabeth Miller-Hall, the prosecutor in charge of handling all the technical arguments for the State. She is the only female involved in trying the case, aside from the seven women on the jury.

Robert Laurino, the director of the Sexual Assault and Rape Analysis Unit of the Essex County Prosecutor's Office.

Glenn Goldberg, who directs the Special Prosecutions Office for Essex County. His singing of "The Sounds of Silence" as he summed up his case against the Glen Ridge rapists is later used by the defense lawyers as one of their grounds for an appeal.

Christopher Archer

Bryant Grober

Kevin Scherzer

Kyle Scherzer

THE JUDGE
Benjamin Cohen, highly rated by his New Jersey peers, dumbfounded critics by allowing the rapists to stay out on bail after their conviction because he worried about mistakes he might have made during the trial.

KEVIN SCHERZER'S LAWYER:
Michael Querques, who gives the case identity with his "boys-will-be-boys" defense. Querques is in private practice in Orange, New Jersey.

KYLE SCHERZER'S LAWYER:
Louis Esposito, who also practices law privately in Orange. Esposito reinforces the reality of Betty's deficiencies by speaking in baby talk to her. "Pretty please," he urges her at the onset of his cross-examination.

CHRISTOPHER ARCHER'S LAWYER:
Thomas Ford, Jr., whose private practice is in Millburn. Ford is proud of his efforts to keep Archer out of prison. "I suppose we went wrong," he tells the the *New Jersey Law Journal* as the guilty verdict sinks in, "in the twelve jurors we picked."

BRYANT GROBER'S LAWYER:
Alan Zegas, whose law shingle hangs in West Orange, New Jersey. He manages to convince the jury that his client committed a less serious crime than the others because he removed himself from the crowd when Betty is violated with a bat, broom, and stick.

NATIONAL ORGANIZATION FOR WOMEN TRIAL OBSERVER:
Carol Vasile, an organizer in the women's movement.

Peter Quigley

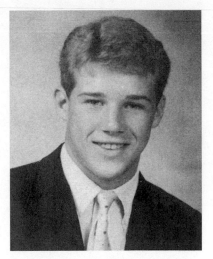

Paul Archer

John Maher

Richard Corcoran

Elizabeth Miller-Hall

Robert Laurino

Glenn Goldberg

Judge Benjamin Cohen

Michael Querques

Louis Esposito

Thomas Ford, Jr.

Alan Zegas

Preface:
"She Wanted It"

None of the rapists charged in the Glen Ridge case stood up and said, "I didn't do it." Not one denied the basic details of the story of their predatory perversion—or their own overt participation in the abuse of their classmate—a story reconstructed here. And that is, perhaps, one of the saddest aspects of the entire sordid Glen Ridge affair.

Despite their self-serving courtroom apologies seconds before they were sentenced by Judge Cohen, the four anti-heroes of the Glen Ridge tragedy justified their attack by insisting that their mentally deficient neighbor was a willing participant in her own abuse. They failed to understand—or refused to accept—their basic moral obligations as civilized human beings. One of the gang, just after the crime became public, brazenly dismissed questions about his involvement with an arrogant, "She wanted it."

The State of New Jersey managed to convince the jury of the rapists' guilt by showing that the victim was not equipped with the mental capacity to consent to the abuse she suffered that miserable afternoon in her neighbors' basement. Nor, the jury agreed, did she understand her right and her potential ability to say no to her attackers. And, in an important expansion of exactly what constitutes rape, the Glen Ridge case established both that the legal definition of force during a sexual assault is not limited to physically overpowering the victim and that criminal threats need not be spoken; they can be implied.

My role here, as reporter and storyteller, is to show how a band of privileged youngsters ended up as conspiring felons and remained unrepentant in court—and to speculate about whether or not their monstrous crimes are isolated criminal aberrations or instead are representative of a greater moral decay pervading much of our struggling and confused society.

This is a true story, and what I present here are the facts of the case. The name of the rapists' victim is no secret. Although Judge Cohen instructed reporters covering the trial not to name the victim and although her name is supposed to be stricken from all court transcripts made public, it is probably impossible to find a soul in Glen Ridge who is not intimately familiar with the details of the case—including the names of all the players. The name of the victim comes out easily and without censorship whenever the case is discussed. Nonetheless, I am convinced that using the correct name of the victim adds nothing to the value of the story I tell here. If by changing her name in this book I potentially protect her and her family from further problems relating to the rape and its aftermath, it is well worth the substitution. So, we will get to know her in these pages as Betty Harris. Hers is the only name changed.

This is a story that starts long before that mournful afternoon in the Scherzer house at 34 Lorraine Street, back when Christopher Archer and the Scherzer twins were in Glen Ridge kindergarten and discovering how much they enjoyed making life more difficult for one of the little neighbor girls.

"She was slower, she was simple," Bart Ciccolini testified about his classmate Betty, a neighbor he had known since he was five years old. Ciccolini managed the Glen Ridge High girls' junior varsity basketball team when Betty was a regular player. Although she knew the team's strategy and played well enough to participate in games, after just a couple of minutes of talking with her, Ciccolini said, "you would know she was slightly retarded. Everybody knew she was slower." Her mental status was part of the community lore for those growing up in the south end of Glen Ridge. She was the one, he said, "everybody teased."

Christine Middleton was the captain of Betty's basketball team. Like all the other Glen Ridge kids who encountered Betty, she knew Betty was mentally inferior to her teammates. "If we told her, 'Guard number twelve,' she would probably follow her out the door," is how Middleton expressed it. Middleton and the other girls laughed at Betty, made jokes about her, teased her. "She would be looking for us when we told her we were playing hide and seek," she testified as an example of how the other players on the team toyed with Betty, "but we would be in the house instead."

"No one wanted to eat with her." Columbia High School counselor Carol Bolden watched as Betty suffered through adolescence. "No one wanted to be around her in the hallways. She was very much isolated. She was in her own little world at times. It was very sad. She was treated as the oddball. She had a real need to be liked. She had a real need to do anything she felt would make a friend."

"People used to come up to me," testified Betty's sister, "and say, 'Your sister's retarded.'" Neighborhood nicknames for Betty were "dummy" and "retarded" and "piggy," she said. She remembered the time a group of girls gathered with her sister at a mud puddle to form make-believe chocolate bars with the mud. Betty and one of the other girls were instructed to eat them. Only Betty complied.

Another time Betty came home with a reddened arm. "They were pinching me," was her explanation. Betty's sister said their father asked Betty why she had not stopped the other children. "I don't know," was the response from Betty.

Betty's sister told the jury that she was sure Betty would do anything anybody asked.

Betty Harris was just five when the Scherzer twins were among the boys who convinced Betty to eat dog feces. The little Scherzers knew back then, despite what defense lawyers tried to convince the jury, that Betty was different, vulnerable, ready to do what they told her to do or asked her to do, and anxious to please them. Christopher Archer learned that same lesson early, too. That's why he was one of the kids who amused themselves during a Glen Ridge summer tennis camp by heckling the eleven-year-old Betty with chants of "retard" and "stupid."

Betty Harris was the south end Glen Ridge town fool.

The Sentencing

T he radio reverberates Howard Stern as I crisscross downtown Newark, making my way to the Essex County Courthouse. It is April 23, 1993—sentencing day for the Glen
Ridge rapists.

Stern is busy titillating his audience again this morning. He's
matched up a couple of listeners—live on the air—for a blind date.
"How far" will the boy get with the girl on this first date? Stern won-
ders aloud over and over again. Will the boy, asks Stern, make it to
"first base? second base? third base?" What are the chances that he
will go "all the way?"

At this point Stern feels that some further explanation is in order:
"That means in her pants," he announces with authority referring
to third base.

"Ing-bray ondoms-kay," Stern tells the boy.

I'm listening to this barrage as I troll past the cheap junk empo-
riums lining Broad Street. I pass the empty Buick dealership, Broad
Gifts and Broad Fast Food, Roberto's Pizza. Newark Bargain Center
and Newark Drugs call out with huge block letters across their
facades. Newark is a blur of garbage in the crumbling streets,
boarded-up vacant buildings, and empty lots gone to seed filled
with trash and the remnants of better Newark days: hunks of rust-
ing Industrial Revolution machinery, chunks of foundation brick,

railroad ties. Colorful, festive-looking banners hang from street lamp posts with a vain cry of *Newark—A City on the Rise.*

"What makes you think I don't carry condoms?" protests the bubbly girl on the other line.

"Are you wild?" Stern asks her, curious if she might "jump in bed" with the boy on this first date. She allows that, although she no longer drinks, she never rules out anything. Stern and his crew lament her sobriety, worrying that it might reduce the boy's odds of a sexual encounter.

I'm looking for a parking space now. Cars line Newark streets, blatantly facing NO PARKING signs. Directly across a side street from a restricted courthouse entrance—the one used by jurors, witnesses, and the accused to escape the crowds—the hulk of a long burned-out single-family home dominates still another trash-filled and overgrown block of vacant lots. Sheet metal tacked over the broken windows clangs with the wind. It is a blustery spring day, cold and overcast.

After a commercial, Howard Stern is back with a long soliloquy, sharing his latest fantasy with New Jersey. It is not yet nine in the morning, Friday. He says he's dreaming about killing his wife and running off to a vacation paradise with a stripper he knows. En route he takes the stripper into the airplane lavatory for sex. He describes what he does with her and to her. The stripper is said to be in the radio studio—naked—with him as he tells this story. She's introduced and says she'd love to join Stern on his vacation.

I'm stopped at a red light. In the car next to me two guys are laughing. From the timing of their grins and comments to each other, it is clear that we're listening to the same radio program. Stern's sidekick—a woman—chortles, too. This is one of the highest-rated radio shows in New Jersey, and all across America.

A crowd of TV trucks lines the sidewalk in front of the courthouse, microwave masts probing the gray sky. Airport-style security blocks the public entrance to what is called the New Courts Building. About two decades old, the same age as the Glen Ridge rapists, it is a gritty utilitarian high-rise with no sense of style, majesty, or particular purpose.

The bored security guards quickly lose their patience with visitors who neglect to empty all the metal from their pockets and so set off the alarm. Soda and ice cream machines light up the jammed lobby. Cops and lawyers join plaintiffs and defendants waiting for the slow, crowded elevators.

The courtroom of Judge R. Benjamin Cohen is on the eighth floor. I stop off in the men's room. It is dirty and smelly, reminiscent of a bus station. The graffiti covering the walls mocks the criminal justice system. "If you have a 1991 Honda Accord it's being stolen now," reads one scrawl, and 1991 is scratched out and replaced with 1992, the Honda year now preferred by Newark's notoriously efficient car thieves. "Viva Columbia," reads another, referring to the cocaine trade. Columbia is spelled wrong and corrected in another handwriting that suggests the original writer go back to school. Another message over one of the urinals: "As you read this your wife is being fuck by me."

I take my seat in Judge Cohen's courtroom. Handwritten signs reserve rows for the press and for family members of the four guilty men. The dull sky is visible through the narrow slits of windows; the wind whines through them too. "I'm surprised this place isn't packed," says the smiling black deputy keeping order. He tells reporters not to eat or drink coffee while we wait for the judge. He wears a bright blue uniform shirt, collar fraying. His gut rolls heavy over a belt already weighed down with his pistol. An American flag is hanging forgotten back in a far corner.

Spectators continue to mill about. One is standing in the first row of seats, talking with another, killing time. The space in the row is narrow and the fellow standing flashes his jacket open and jokes about the juxtaposition of his crotch and the other man's mouth.

The rapists walk in: grim, beefy, and dressed in stylish well-tailored suits or coats, ties, and slacks. They wear the clothing well, easily. One is chewing gum; the chatty deputy motions for him to remove it. Directly behind the four, in the family members' section, sits a row of girls about the same age as the four men. They look like caricatures of New Jersey girls. Their hair is teased, colored, and curled. They play with it. They wear too much makeup. Several chew gum.

For more than an hour lawyers make arguments and counter-arguments for a summary judgment of acquittal. The four guilty men sit through it all with no sign of emotion; somber or arrogant, they rarely exchange a word or gesture with each other.

Judge Cohen calmly recites his rationale as he prepares to announce his decision. He identifies the rape as an "especially heinous, cruel, and degrading" crime because a baseball bat, broom handle, and stick were used during the attack. He calls it a "group show" and a "spectacle" because of the audience of thirteen boys who watched the assault. He notes the physical and emotional harm done to the mentally retarded victim. But the judge also acknowledges the rapists' youth at the time of the crime, their lack of prior "substantial criminal records," and his belief that they are sorry for their actions.

One by one the guilty men are offered a chance to speak before they hear their fate. Throughout the five months of trial, not one of them has testified or talked with reporters, and their lawyers still advise them to stay quiet.

"I think I've remained silent too long," says Christopher Archer—standing with still no visible sign of emotion. He remains composed as he speaks, using a strong, steady voice. "I'm sorry, " he says. "I'm sorry [for the victim]. I never intended for this to happen." It was Archer who lured the victim to his friends' basement—the "mastermind" of the crime a prosecutor calls him—with the promise of a later date with his older brother. "I ask you to let me learn from my mistake," he says, pleading for leniency. Archer's lawyer paints his client as a victim: "We don't want him to re-enter [society] as a hardened individual based on what he'd learn in prison."

Next to speak is Bryant Grober. The other three men are guilty of sexual assault, Grober only of conspiracy. He knows as he stands that it is unlikely the judge will send him to prison. He is praised by his lawyer as a skilled lifeguard along the Jersey Shore, a sympathetic man who helps cripples down the beach to the water. "All of us in our lives," pleads the lawyer, "make mistakes, Your Honor, and Bryant has been punished." The prosecutor is unimpressed. "He engaged in the first sexual act," Robert Laurino reminds the judge.

"He was the one who started the fire. What did he do to save [the victim] as she went down for the third time?"

Grober's voice quivers slightly as he addresses the court. "Over the past four years I've done a lot of thinking. It was wrong, stupid," he says about the crime. "It should never have happened. I can't express the sorrow I feel. I made a mistake. I've apologized to my parents many times." He announces that he has yet to apologize to his victim and her parents and asks the judge to pass along his concern.

The gum-chewing row of Jersey women is paying attention again. During the legal arguments that filled most of the morning, their eyes were glazed over or wandering around the courtroom. They held each other's hands or whispered back and forth. They played with their hair. They tried to look as if they were listening and comprehending. They draw my attention, and I'm not alone. One reporter writes on her notebook, "What do you think the total IQ is on that bench behind the defendants?" She passes the note over to another newswoman, and they nod in agreement and smile.

Kevin Scherzer rises next. It was in his basement that he and his twin brother, Kyle, joined their high school football star friends to violate their mentally deficient neighbor, a childhood classmate. "I'm very sorry for what happened." His voice is strong. "I used bad moral judgment at the time," he explains. "I was very young." He apologizes to his family and to the victim's family. "I'm just sorry about everything." He sits down, and his brother declines to speak. But prosecutor Laurino reminds the judge that it was Kyle who put a plastic bag on the bat before it was introduced into the victim, "not to protect the victim," his voices rises, "but to protect the bat!"

Laurino makes one more attempt to influence the judge: "This was violence, not sex. There was no sexual gratification." He again brings up the victim's mental deficiencies. "Did they pick a normal girl?" he asks and answers the question for himself. "No. They knew a normal girl would not tolerate it. They knew their girlfriends would not tolerate it." Laurino concludes his plea with an attack on a defense suggestion that the victim is uninjured. "To say a woman who is raped is not harmed is an insult to women. Society was a victim in that basement." He is unimpressed with the apologies he hears. "They are not sorry for the victim, but sorry for themselves and the situation they got themselves into."

One of the blondes in the second row of seats shakes her head and rolls her eyes in disgust at the prosecutor's speech. But he is not quite finished.

"To try to cast these boys as all-American boys," he says, his voice rising again, "is an insult to boys in America. The eyes of this country are on this court. People are captivated and repulsed by this case. These rapists must be deterred from senseless acts of sexual violence."

"I'm sorry to be here and sorry for Betty Harris's family, who had to endure this," says Judge Cohen as he reads his decisions. Bryant Grober gets the expected probation; the other three get indeterminate sentences not to exceed fifteen years—but prison time that could be end up to be as little as a couple of years—about the same as the average time convicted rapists serve nationwide. They are to serve their time in a prison reserved for what New Jersey calls "youthful offenders." There is no noticeable reaction from the four as the sentences are read. Then, in a step that outrages the watching world, the judge agrees to a defense request that the criminals remain free on bail while their lawyers file appeals—a process that can stretch out for years.

The girls in the second row sob and wipe tears from their eyes.

"HOW DARE HE!" screams the *New York Post* later that evening across its front page, quoting Christine McGoey, who observed the entire trial for the National Organization for Women. "This judge has sold women out," she insists. Her colleague, Carol Vasile, denounces the sentence as showing "if you're wealthy, you're white, and you're educated, then you're allowed to rape and get away with it. It's a blow to women today." They are just two parts in a chorus of upset and frustration. The *New York Times* adds its voice in an editorial a few days later, charging that "justice isn't color-blind. When it comes to crime, it seems, there's still nothing like being white, middle-class, and suburban to get you the benefit of the doubt." The Essex County prosecutor says he's "shocked and appalled," calling the sentence "lenient treatment afforded to convicted rapists" and criticizing

Judge Cohen for making "a mistake." In court, assistant prosecutor Glenn Goldberg implores the judge to send Archer and the Scherzer twins directly to prison. "There is no justification to excuse this conduct," he says in an intense voice, "because to do so would be to say, 'Boys will be boys.'" And, outside the courtroom, Paul Scherzer, the twins' older brother, complains too, calling the sentences "very harsh." Pleased that his brothers will remain out of prison during the appeals process, he complains nonetheless about the potential fifteen years behind bars: "I don't think it served justice in this case."

The elevators cannot handle the throng. I find the staircase and meander down, considering the sentences, the case, our culture. I hear footsteps racing behind me. Christopher Archer is using the same shortcut, hurtling down the stairs—still not talking much. "Excuse me," is all he says as he and his buddies head once again back to their affluent Glen Ridge enclave.

In the lobby of the courthouse, a black woman pauses to watch the crowd of reporters and cameras. She turns away from the harsh lights and the explanatory statements coming from the lawyers. "If they were black," she says with disgust, dismissal, and resignation, "if they were black, they'd be in jail."

A Promised Date

etty Harris was alone at the Carteret Field playground on the south side of Glen Ridge when Christopher Archer approached her that first day of March in 1989. She was seventeen years old but with an IQ measured at only sixty-four—her intellectual abilities and social skills operated at roughly the level of an average eight-year-old girl. She was dribbling her basketball, shooting at the hoop.

"No!" Betty answered firmly when Archer asked her to come with him and his friends over to the Scherzer twins' house across the street, where only the Scherzers' grandmother was home. Betty said she was not interested in leaving the park.

Christopher was insistent. He said he had a prize for Betty if she would agree to join him and some friends at the Scherzer house. He promised her a date later that night with his brother Paul. With an arm around her, Christopher further encouraged Betty, finally convincing her, leading her up into the Scherzer house and then down into the finished and furnished basement.

"It was romantic," she would remember later as she tried to sort out the day's events, "because he had his arm around me." The romance was short lived. She was positioned on a couch, surrounded by Christopher, his brother Paul, Kyle and Kevin Scherzer, the Glen Ridge police lieutenant's son Richard Corcoran, Peter

A Question of Consent

Quigley, Bryant Grober, and a half dozen more of their teammates.

With the boys watching closely, the attack started. "It was set up like a movie," Betty would recall about the arrangement of the chairs in the basement. "The way they looked at me, like I was sup- posed to do it, like a movie." From the text of the indictment, to Betty's and Paul Archer's testimony, to the memory of some of the witnesses who were not charged with any crime, the exact details and the order of their progression differ somewhat. But the basic scenario is consistent no matter who is recounting the tragedy, a basic scenario never denied by the defendants.

First Bryant Grober joined Betty on the couch and pulled down his jeans and his underwear. After Christopher, Kevin, and Peter Quigley told Betty to remove her clothes, Christopher and Grober undressed her or she was induced to remove her sweat suit herself. Next, says the indictment, Grober "received fellatio" from Betty. Then he pushed her "head further down onto his penis." In the audience, Christopher Archer laughed, the other friends laughed, and Archer yelled, "Go further, go further!" A few months later, Betty would tell a psychologist that the experience with Grober was "gross" but that it didn't "bother her." She would explain her involvement with these words: "I didn't want to put him down. It would be putting him down not to do it."

Soon Grober had enough. He slunk away from the couch and hung his head in his hands, while Christopher kept the cheering section going, asking Betty if "she swallowed cum."

Betty was in a daze and followed instructions to masturbate her- self. "Put five fingers up your vagina," Betty remembers they told her. "Finger yourself," called out Bryant Grober. And she did. The police- man's son, Richard Corcoran, and the promised date, Paul Archer, asked Betty, "How does it feel?" The indictment says Christopher went past just the question and "inserted his fingers into [Betty's] vagina."

"Then came the broomstick," Betty recounted later in court. Kyle Scherzer "got plastic bags and some Vaseline," said prosecutor Glenn Goldberg during his opening argument, "and he put bags over some of these instruments, these wooden objects, and spread the Vaseline over them." The objects were the broomstick and other implements still to come. "It may not be entirely clear exactly why he did it," Goldberg remarked about the Vaseline, "whether it was to make it easier for these other perpetrators to get the sticks in, whether in part it was to protect Betty, whether in part to protect the broom and the bat, so they wouldn't pick up any substances or materials—but what he did was part and parcel of the crimes of aiding and abetting in the penetration."

Kevin took the covered and lubricated broom from his twin and, testified Betty, "stuck it into me." The cheering section responded with more shouts of, "Go further, go further!" and the boys laughed. Kevin took hold of the bristle end of the broom, pushed it further into Betty, and then spent the next couple of minutes manipulating the broom—shifting it in and out of Betty. He wasn't alone. Christopher grabbed the broom and pushed and pulled too.

"Then came the bat," says Betty. Kyle carefully covered his practice bat with a protective plastic bag and lubricated it. It was a fungo bat—used for fielding practice—thirty-three inches long, with a two-inch diameter at the handle and measuring an inch and three-quarters across the end. "Put it up further," coaxed Peter Quigley, say the prosecutors. "Put it up further! Does it make you feel good?"

"Stick it up her further," suggested Corcoran. More laughter from the group and some catcalls. "Whore!" called out one of Betty's tormentors as she endured the pain.

At that point, some of the gang assaulting Betty got nervous. Some in the back of the throng had already drifted out of the basement. "I felt uncomfortable," Philip Grant would later explain to jurors. "I didn't want any part of group sex." Nor did he want to testify against his friends. "It's hard for me to say to this day why I left. I didn't feel something wrong was going on. I didn't feel like I should be there." Grant left soon after Bryant Grober pulled down his pants, and Philip Grant—like several members of the cheering section—was not charged with any crime.

Bart Ciccolini, the manager of Betty's basketball team, left as Grober's pants went down, too. Ciccolini saw Betty's sweat pants pulled down at about the same time, and "I noticed something wasn't right there." Ciccolini would later tell investigators that it was Christopher Archer who convinced Betty to take off her pants, a deduction, he would testify at the trial, that he arrived at because of the "puzzled" and "skeptical" look on her face.

With the bat still inside Betty, Kyle Scherzer called out to his brother, "Stop, you're hurting her!" But Kevin continued to manipulate the bat. Kyle, forgetting his concern, next found and lubricated an old dowel stick, and the assault continued with the stick, described by investigators as "dirty."

Neither Christopher Archer nor Kevin Scherzer were finished. They both sucked Betty's breasts, and one of their buddies yelled out, "You can go when one of us comes!" In turn Betty masturbated Richard Corcoran, Christopher and Paul Archer, Peter Quigley, and Bryant Grober. Finally Kevin Scherzer was masturbated, and he ejaculated.

Betty was told she could leave the basement—but not to tell anyone what had just happened to her. If she revealed their secret, her mother would be informed and she would be expelled from school. Prosecutor Goldberg paraphrased what the stunned victim was told: "Betty, what happened today is a secret, just between you and us, and it is not something for you to discuss with anyone. In fact, we will engage now in a secret pact. You and we boys will have a secret pact, we will sort of shake hands on it, put our hands together, and we will all agree among ourselves that we won't talk about what happened here with anybody."

Betty agreed that she would never tell anyone about the attack. Kyle Scherzer took charge. "You can go now," he told Betty, and she climbed out of the Scherzer basement.

That night there would be no date with Paul Archer, just pain. "It hurt when I went to the bathroom," Betty later reported. She told one of her few true friends that the assault "was a terrible thing." Still to come would be the nightmares, the appetite loss, and the guilt, manifesting itself as worry that she was the cause of trouble suffered by her friends the attackers.

The
Rich
White
Suburb

J ust seven miles up Bloomfield Avenue from the misery of
Newark is the luxury of Glen Ridge—by all outward appearances a charmed community. Ridgers are proud of their
lineage, tracing their common heritage back to 1666 and a
land purchase from the Yantecaw Indians. Along Bloomfield
Avenue, the decay of Newark quickly gives way to thriving Italian
restaurants, car dealerships, and the slightly less urban bustle of the
town of Bloomfield.

Family-style businesses still outnumber franchise outlets in
Bloomfield. Giannotto's Pharmacy and Vesuvius Restaurant and
Bar share the typical American small-town neighborhood with
Michelangelo's Seafood, R & S Strauss Auto Parts, and Castelli Bros.
Bakery. A handful of teenagers struggle with the video game at the
Nevada Diner. An older man walks in and instructs them, "Just
break the fucking machine and do it right."

Across the street, the Town Pub's neon sign calls out to Bloomfield and Glen Ridge residents looking for a drink and a party. This
is where the Scherzer twins, Christopher Archer, and their friends
go to find a beer and a sympathetic ear.

On any given evening, the mood in the bar is typical of a suburban pick-up joint. "You look like somebody famous." John, one of
the Town Pub regulars, uses the tired line on a new girl in town one

Thursday night soon after the sentencing. She suggests some curiosity. He looks puzzled and then proceeds with satisfaction, "I've got it! Drew Barrymore!" John is an athletic man in his early twenties, at home in the bar setting and confident as he addresses the stranger.

Next his friend Sean makes a move on another single woman. "Did I tell you I lost my MAC card?" he asks her. Automatic teller machine cards are known as MAC cards in New Jersey.

"Yeah, three times." She's more interested in being compared with Barrymore than in hearing about Sean's problems.

"I probably did," acknowledges Sean and goes on to tell her again.

Brad, another regular, talks about a mutual friend not at the bar. "It's like Mickey," says Brad. "He doesn't get hung over—sometimes he just gets a little sober."

"Did you hear what they did to Mickey?" John asks his pals. "From point-blank range they threw darts at his butt. And when they pulled them out, they had to really pull." John demonstrates for his audience.

"The guy is a human being," Brad says, protesting what happened to Mickey.

"It's funny," suggests John, "but it wouldn't be funny to watch."

The banter and atmosphere create a comfortable scene for the convicted rapists. They feel at home hanging out in places like the Town Pub—extensions of the bawdy environments they enjoyed at Glen Ridge High and in their family dens and recreation rooms.

■

A startling change occurs when crossing the line from Bloomfield into Glen Ridge. The shift from a working-class business district to wealth is stark and immediate. Suddenly many of the houses are gracious and huge, the lawns sprawl under well-established shade trees, and the trademark Glen Ridge gaslights flicker through the nights on all the corners.

Many Ridgers trace the sense of insular independence that they enjoy to their secession from Bloomfield. By the 1890s, discontent was brewing in the Hill section of Bloomfield. Equitable distribution of tax monies was the issue. The Ridgers looked at their unpaved streets and the lack of public water distribution and sewers; they concluded that they were not being treated fairly and decided to separate from the flatlanders.

Glen Ridge histories cite the secessionist mentality as a pivotal element in the development of the character of Glen Ridge. "The citizens felt they were faced with the classic taxation without repre- sentation," explains Ronald Tavisano in *Glen Ridge*, a popular history of the borough. "The stage was set and the independence movement began in earnest." The zeal that Ridgers feel for their independence is of the type usually reserved for nationhood. Tavisano declares, "It is clear that the independence movement might not have occurred had it not been for a certain group of men, the Borough's Found- ing Fathers. These men were not unlike many of our nation's founders. They were men of substance, financially comfortable, distinguished in their careers, ready to serve the public interest as they perceived it and to take any risk entailed." Newspaper reporters during secession were even more enthralled, bowing to the found- ing fathers as "the patriarchs of exodus."

Life improved after secession. The outhouses were hauled away, replaced by a modern municipal water and sewer system. Gathering dust in the Glen Ridge Library is long-time Ridger Clarence Graham's account of the boyhood he enjoyed growing up on High- land Avenue, a hundred years before the Scherzer twins, Christo- pher Archer, Bryant Grober, and the rest of their gang decided to get their kicks raping their neighbor.

He and his friends passed hot summer afternoons swimming in the Morris Canal. "Once in a while," wrote Graham, "a rival gang would appear and then we were subject to some rather unfair tactics. Sometimes as we were emerging from the water to dress, somebody would throw a couple of handfuls of dirt in the air which would settle on our damp shoulders, compelling us to go back and wash off. Another trick they had was to 'chaw' our clothes. Trans- lated this meant tying knots in our underwear and stockings. We were quite chilled at times before we could get them undone." Other antics Graham remembers from those early Glen Ridge days included taking a short cut through a neighbor's field even though the farmer had ordered them to stay away from his corn.

■

For the next hundred years Glen Ridge grew, and the Ridgers prospered. Residents work hard to maintain their privileged way of life and even adjusted the traditional American political system in their continuing efforts to keep the rest of the world at bay. In 1913, under the guise of protecting Glen Ridgers from the evils of multiparty politics, the chairmen of the local Democratic and Republican parties joined with other political and business leaders to form an organization still unique to New Jersey politics, the Civic Conference Committee. By design, they created an ironclad grip by the existing social and business establishment on the government of their town, a one-party system guaranteeing the perpetuation of the social status quo and the exclusion from town politics of any outsiders promoting viewpoints that differed from those of the "patriarchs of exodus."

Here is how the committee, known in Glen Ridge simply as the CCC, works. Delegates are elected for three-year terms by the civic groups that make up the committee. These delegates sit on a board that selects candidates for political office, candidates to be endorsed by the CCC. Eleven different organizations, such as the Women's Club, the North Side Association, and the Taxpayers Association, have achieved the status required of CCC members— the CCC itself decides what types and which specific clubs can join the CCC. Groups that gather solely for athletic, religious, business, literary, or even social purposes are supposedly precluded from membership in the CCC. Member organizations must be active in political matters. Especially in a small town, distinguishing exactly what constitutes political action as opposed to strictly social activity is completely subjective. By its own definitions, the CCC makes these distinctions arbitrarily.

The delegates elected by these member organizations convene as the Civic Conference Committee with the mandate to accomplish just one chore: the selection of the slate of CCC-endorsed candidates for upcoming elections. Delegates, in secret, interview prospective candidates for office—supposedly without concern for political affiliation. They interview, again in private, references for those candidates. Then, once again behind closed doors and with all delegates sworn to secrecy, the committee debates the pros and cons of the candidates interviewed and makes its choices for endorsement.

Of course, since Glen Ridge is in the United States, other candidates may try to get on the ballot and run for office without CCC endorsement. But since the CCC is made up of delegates from member organizations that control most of the money in town and wield most of the social and political influence, it is difficult for independent operators to fight city hall. In fact, since the CCC was established in 1913, except for a handful of elections, only CCC candidates have managed to triumph at the polls.

A few contested elections have been close calls for a CCC-endorsed candidate. But only a few. Usually the CCC candidates run unopposed. Once in a while, write-in candidates manage to get a few votes. The Democrats, unlike the Republicans, no longer participate in the CCC cabal and periodically send a candidate into the fray. But the CCC nearly always wins, and it is nearly always a landslide.

"The office seeks the man," proclaims a Civic Conference Committee propaganda poster from one of the few contested elections, a 1954 school board race. The poster is titled "A Threat to the Foundation of Our Town!" and its text and tone offer a disturbing defense of CCC rule.

"We don't have rough and tumble, knock 'em down and drag 'em out political campaigns in our town! And we do have good government and good schools. Now, a group seeks to inject partisan politics into the picture." The group in question was the Democratic party. "The group," continues the polemic, "formerly a full partner in the Civic Conference Committee, voluntarily staged a 'walkout' in 1948. It surrendered its right to participate in Glen Ridge government of its own accord. Yet its leaders have advanced their slate of candidates for the three Board of Education posts. The possible result is all too clear. Unless this maneuver is rejected overwhelmingly, Glen Ridge will be in danger of succumbing to something that is wrecking sound home life, good schools, and good government in too many communities: partisan politics."

The tirade concludes, "We think Glen Ridge is a fine place to live. It's a hundred to one that you do, too! It's a friendly town. Let's keep it that way, by keeping partisan politics out. Protect your town from politics. Be sure to vote." The CCC candidates won.

Proponents of this bizarre arrangement point to its virtues with pride, claiming that it avoids the kind of divisive infighting that can be so destructive and counterproductive, especially in a small town like Glen Ridge, where politics can pit neighbor against neighbor and engender long-lasting feuds. Advocates of the CCC method of selecting candidates also remain convinced that their interview process connects the best possible available candidates with the elective offices up for grabs. They claim that since the system is supposedly nonpartisan and because elective positions in Glen Ridge government—the mayor, the city council, and the school board—pay nothing, candidates are motivated only by public service.

Critics of this closed system see it otherwise, of course. To them the CCC is a slick device that the establishment uses to control the town for its own selfish purposes. Residents who do not participate in the activities of one of the clubs that send delegates to the CCC enjoy little chance of ever attaining a public office. Perhaps even worse, by the rules of what the CCC calls its constitution, a Glen Ridger who is not a member—either by personal choice or because of exclusion—of one of the organizations providing the CCC with delegates enjoys no direct method of influencing the CCC endorsements.

This closed and elitist system of government, developed and perpetuated by a paranoid small-town society, institutionalized Glen Ridge's "us-against-them" mentality, a mentality that made it easy to protect the town's athletic stars from outside criticism.

■

Glen Ridge nurtures athletes. High school sports heroes are treasured by the community. The year before Betty Harris was raped, Glen Ridge High's baseball and basketball teams were New Jersey state champions. The Glen Ridge High School football team is a local legend, proud of a long winning streak in the late sixties and early seventies. The 1958 team was quarterbacked by Gary Cuozzo, an honor student who went on to captain the University of Virginia team and play professional football for both the Baltimore Colts and the Minnesota Vikings. Now a dentist practicing near the old neighborhood, Cuozzo maintains his star status in Glen Ridge.

The Scherzer twins and their buddies inherited this tradition when Kevin and Kyle took over as cocaptains of the 1988 Glen Ridge High football squad. But the team performed poorly, winning only two games all season, and one of those was an empty victory—an opposing team forfeited. The four convicted Glen Ridge rapists all played football together that year and were busy with baseball when they attacked Betty Harris. Off the field, their teachers were less than impressed with the players. Just after charges were filed against them, *New York Times* reporter Lisa Foderaro talked about their school careers with Kathleen Blakeley, the president of the Glen Ridge Middle School Home and School Association. "These were troubled kids all along," Blakeley remembered. "They were always rowdy—the kind of trouble you always have with kids who have some athletic prowess but nothing going in their lives except that. They don't respect learning. They don't respect teachers. There's a different ethos that takes place when they are in a group than when they are alone."

But so many of the townspeople felt they needed high school sports successes and athletic heroes for a sense of civic pride and satisfaction, that the rowdiness was nurtured, too. According to news interviews with local civic leaders, Glen Ridge police tended to look the other way or offer just a slap on the wrist when they encountered errant sports stars.

The connection between the Glen Ridge establishment and the town's outlaw sports subculture could be seen early on as the rape case unfolded publicly. Three months after the initial charges were filed, prosecutors added another defendant to the list of alleged rapists: Richard Corcoran. Corcoran, whose case eventually was separated from that of the Scherzer twins, Christopher Archer, and Bryant Grober, was also a Glen Ridge High football player. But he had another crucial link to the town. His father was the Glen Ridge Police Department lieutenant in charge of the department's detectives. Initially, Lieutenant Corcoran was in charge of the investigation into the rape of Betty Harris.

Lieutenant Corcoran was removed from the case once it was determined by other investigators that his son was involved in the crime. But since rumor and gossip around Glen Ridge had long before placed the younger Corcoran at the scene of the crime, critics and cynics suspected the lieutenant of trying to protect his son from criminal charges that can carry as much as thirty-five years in prison and $207,500 in fines.

Essex County prosecutor Herbert Tate tried to avoid tainting the credibility of the Glen Ridge Police Department and its chief of detectives. "The fact that charges have been filed against Richard Corcoran, Jr.," he announced, "in no way implies that the Glen Ridge Police Department committed any impropriety in connection with the investigation."

Just a few months earlier it was the younger Corcoran who had responded to a question about the case with the terse, "She wanted it." Now—with his father no longer directly involved in the case—the indictment against him charged that he said, "Stick it up her further," while one of the foreign objects was being manipulated inside Betty Harris's vagina, and that he inserted the dirty dowel stick into her.

■

Cover-ups—or at least foot-dragging—were also suspected at the high school. Betty was attacked March 1, 1989. Three days later she told her swimming instructor about the crime. "She didn't just run up to Margaret Savage and blurt out the whole thing," prosecutor Glenn Goldberg explained as he recounted Betty's first report of the crime. "She sort of sounded her out a little bit. She gradually hinted at something that had happened—sort of a party, the party involving young men, but something she didn't want to talk about."

Margaret Savage was well trained in teaching handicapped children and in counseling. She sensed that something serious was amiss. She made arrangements with Betty to get together the next day and convinced Betty to share her upset. Again, Goldberg picks up the story: "Sure enough, the next day when they were together, Betty began to tell more, not everything, not all the details, not even accurately, everything that had happened to her."

Betty did not seek out her teacher to expose the boys who raped her so viciously. "She had no intention of betraying the boys," said Goldberg. "The boys, you see, were her friends. She wouldn't do anything to hurt these boys. She wouldn't tell anybody to get the boys in trouble. The reason Betty told Mrs. Savage what happened is because she wanted to know how to say no if she ever got caught in that type of situation again."

"She asked me, 'How do I say no if this happens again?'" Margaret Savage testified when she was called to the witness stand during the trial.

Betty Harris did not go to high school with her attackers; she attended nearby Columbia High School and West Orange High School to take advantage of special classes for the mentally retarded, classes not offered in Glen Ridge. Within a week after the rape, a social worker told Betty's mother what the swim teacher had heard from Betty. At first her mother did not believe the charges. Because of the mother's disbelief, the social worker said later that she felt no obligation to inform Glen Ridge High School administrators or the police.

But stories about the rape were all over the Glen Ridge campus— the rapists were bragging and the gossipers were spreading their tale. At least one teacher overheard and ignored the stories. By the middle of March, senior Charles Figueroa formally complained to school officials about the rapists, saying they asked him to join them for a second session with Betty, one they wanted Charles to videotape. It was the second time he tried to force the school to respond,

Charles said later—the first time was just a couple of days after the rape. Through his lawyer, Figueroa passed the word to news reporters that when he first reported the incident to school officials, they were skeptical about his claim. When he made his second report, he said he was advised not to report the request for video-taping to the police.

By March 22, Glen Ridge High School principal Michael Buonomo finally stopped hoping the stories would go away, and he called the police. The principal claimed that was the first day he was made aware of the rumors. "We called the police ten minutes later," concludes his report. Although Buonomo and his staff were exon-erated by the Board of Education of any legal wrongdoing for their tardiness, the investigator who studied the school's response for the board advises the obvious: "Doubt should be resolved by reporting rather than not reporting."

The Board of Education study was conducted by retired New Jersey Superior Court Judge Samuel Larner, hired by the board to investigate the school's handling of the charges against its star athletes. The board initially insisted that Larner was completely without connection to the school district. But, in fact, the eighty-year-old judge was recommended for the investigator's job by one of the lawyers who represents the school board, and Larner was paid $5,000 by the board for his work.

There was a fifteen-day delay, found the judge, between the first word a Glen Ridge High teacher heard about the attack and the first call Principal Buonomo made to the police. But he was adamant in his finding that there was no attempt by the school at a cover-up.

"Anti-social conduct crops up from time to time among those brought up in fine families and exposed to a good education," the judge wrote in his report, struggling to understand the crime. "Whether it may arise from a laissez faire upbringing at home or from character deficiencies of the students themselves or from other causes beyond identification, it is manifestly preposterous to place the blame at the footsteps of the school house." Indeed, the judge found fault—as would friends of the rapists and their lawyers later—with the victim's family. "After all," wrote Larner, "the paramount responsibility to report the incident to police authorities rested with the parents of the victim, who were apprised of the facts as far as they were known by school personnel. Their decision not to proceed in that fashion, though understandable in their desire to protect their child, served as the cause for the delay in reporting by the school personnel."

■

The history of Glen Ridge, the structure of its political system, the insular nature of the Glen Ridge social environment, the privileges experienced by its children—especially its star athletes—all contribute to the development of the personalities raised in this little slice of New Jersey. But, as is the case anywhere, anytime, the citizens of the community are personally responsible for their actions. "I don't think that you can really attribute this to Glen Ridge," prosecutor Glenn Goldberg said about blame for the crime after the trial was over. "I think it's the individuals involved." For Goldberg, the exclusive venue of the crime shows that such antisocial activity "can happen in New York, it can happen in New Jersey. It can happen in an urban setting, it can happen in a suburban setting. I imagine it can probably happen in the wilderness, too. I don't think that much can be attributed to the fact that they lived within the borders of Glen Ridge instead of outside the borders of Glen Ridge."

For Goldberg, prosecuting a reprehensible crime committed by vicious criminals was more important than trying to figure out what aspects of their upbringing may have contributed to their aberrant behavior.

4.

A Slow Investigation

T he rain held back on June 28, 1989, as ninety-seven Glen Ridge High School seniors tried to pretend that their graduation was simply a traditional and typical rite of passage. In Glen Ridge, caps and gowns are not the costumes for graduates. The women receive their diplomas wearing white gowns and carrying flowers, the men in white dinner jackets and black slacks. The rest of the trappings were all in place, too. The band played "Pomp and Circumstance," the toga party decorations were already sparkling at the country club (the decadence of Rome was chosen by the student body as the theme for their graduation fling), and most of the speeches were irrelevant.

"The power of parenting still prevails over the power of peers," declared the Reverend Randall Leisey as he thanked the assembled parents for doing such a good job of raising the next generation of Glen Ridgers. The rapists were not in the audience to hear. Eighty-five seniors signed a petition demanding that their accused class-mates be allowed to make the decision to attend or not themselves, but in a deal worked out between school authorities and parents, the star athletes were quietly given their diplomas privately. Some of the rapists' pals considered wearing yellow armbands to show support for the accused during the graduation ceremony. They did not stage their protest, but—in the spirit of another common New

Jersey tradition—the main entrance of Glen Ridge High School was decorated with spray-painted graffiti. "Congrats Pete, Kyle, Kevin," it called out. "We love you."

One of the most impassioned speeches at the graduation came from senior Josh Golin, who directly addressed the crisis he and his town were facing. "All we had to do was pick up the newspapers and read about what a bad class we are," he complained. What about all the good students? he wondered. "I know that every one of the members of the class of '89 has the potential to succeed. After all, if we passed English, we can do anything."

But before the ceremony, Josh spent time with *Rolling Stone* magazine writer Peter Wilkinson, helping explain that bad class. "Certain kids and their parents," Josh told Wilkinson, "they're the privileged ones. It's the jocks, and they come from the wealthier families, and they all belong to the country club." Not only do Glen Ridge student athletes flout the law, complained Josh, but they lead bizarre sex lives.

"First they all started watching porno movies every day after school as freshmen," Josh continued to Wilkinson. "If you can get beer," he explained, "you can get pornos."

The clique of athletes that the Scherzers, the Archers, and the others involved in the crime formed entertained themselves by "getting voyeurs on each other," as one senior explained it to Wilkinson. "Watching people go with each other," a junior explained the terminology. "Hide behind the bed and watch," another student said. "At parties and shit like that," the junior told Wilkinson, "there'd be like ten guys in the closet watching."

Josh was with his friend Willie as he tried to explain the crime that will follow the Glen Ridge Class of 1989 throughout their lives, and Willie came up with a direct correlation between the pornographic movie binges and the rape. "They wanted one [a pornographic movie] for themselves. They had a girl who was open sexually and who was retarded, and so they did it. They didn't realize it was wrong. Now they do."

"They didn't think it was something they should hush up," Josh said. Not that he agreed. "There was fuckin' thirteen of them there when they did this thing!" Wilkinson reported that Josh was angry and getting angrier. "The whole thing kind of reflects what's wrong with this town." Like most of his classmates, Josh spent plenty of time and effort trying to come to terms with the rape. "There were signs that this could happen. Their parents were kind of in the dark. If you looked at what the kids had been doing, you could see that this might be the next step. Most of them are still in the dark. It makes me kind of sad."

Little remains secret at Glen Ridge High School. Most of the students grew up together, and adolescents love to gossip. Word of the assault leaked because the boys in the basement were bragging around school and around town about what they had done to Betty. The story offended many students not absorbed with the athletic stardom of the rapists. One of them posted signs around school reading MOLESTERS AMONG US and HA! HA! YOU JOCKS'LL FINALLY KNOW WHAT IT FEELS LIKE WHEN YOU GET RAPED IN JAIL!

■

A couple of months after the rape, John Miller, a reporter working for the New York television station WNBC, broke the story out of the incestuous confines of Glen Ridge. The first arrests followed his TV report. At that point the Glen Ridge establishment started to question itself. When did the school teachers and administration know something might be wrong, and what did they do about it? Why were the police so slow to act? Was the investigation jeopardized because one of the accused was the son of the detective in charge of the case? And did the sports-crazed community look the other way as its athletes grew up breaking school rules and state laws?

■

Michael Buonomo looked out over the graduates and their families, relieved that his toughest year as Glen Ridge High School principal was finally coming to an end. "They were a different class when they graduated than when they first came in," he said later in one of the most superficial overstatements heard during the entire case. "The class of '89 faced adversity and they overcame it."

A crowd of reporters and photographers watched from the sidelines. Josh was among the graduates who heaved water balloons at them, but the frustration with the messengers had been building in the neighborhood since TV reporter Miller first reported the rape story the month before. Principal Buonomo suggested reporters were to blame for the slipping final grades of some of his students, and Glen Ridge Mayor Edward Callahan complained of a "literal invasion by the national news media." Callahan told his constituents during his Memorial Day speech, "We have also seen the name of our town unfairly treated as being part of this horrendous alleged act."

As the investigation dragged on through June, a frustrated citizen complained to the Glen Ridge city council that she was "tired of the publicity" and insisted that if she needed "a permit to assemble, the press needs one." She wanted Mayor Callahan and the council to use their influence to muzzle the press, to keep reporters out of her town. The *Glen Ridge Paper* responded with an editorial explaining the First Amendment to her and all the other Glen Ridgers who were complaining about their town's tawdry press clippings. "Many residents," it read, "upset because they fear the reputation of this town will be tarnished, want the press to go away. They blame the press for sensationalizing the incident. They say the press is blowing the story out of proportion. Keep in mind, we don't make the news. We just report it."

■

Four years later, shortly after his classmates were sentenced for their crime, I caught up with Josh at his parents' home on the north side of Glen Ridge. They live in a comfortable two-story frame house down the hill and across the Conrail tracks from the mansions sprawling along Ridgewood Avenue. Josh was lounging through the summer before finishing his undergraduate studies in English at the University of Delaware and insisted to me on the telephone that he was not interested in talking any more about the case.

"The *Rolling Stone* thing, it got to be too big a thing in my life," he complained. But he agreed to a meeting, and as we sat in the living room, he conceded that no further difficulties would develop for him if he talked more about his infamous last year at high school.

"I don't feel comfortable around here, ever since the *Rolling Stone* article." Josh speaks softly, his voice expressing resignation to a fate he felt he long ago lost control of. "I feel like these people don't like me." He is referring to the rapists and their supporters. "I feel like I shouldn't care because look who they are. But I still care and that's been the hardest thing for me to deal with, feeling that I still want to be liked by these people, but I know that I shouldn't care because these are people who have done this or people who defend this. I should be secure enough that it doesn't matter that they don't like me."

As we talk, a slight breeze works through a window pushed halfway up the sash. Full shade trees loom over the house. The worst of the midday summer heat stays outside. Josh sinks into the couch next to the piano, relaxed in cutoffs, bare feet, and a T-shirt festooned with Old Glory. Instead of stars, baseballs fill the blue field, and under the flag is the legend "America's Pastime." His hair is cut short, and his complexion almost clear.

When word of the rape first spread through the grapevine of intimate Glen Ridge High, Betty was portrayed as a willing participant in a sexual encounter with the school's football heroes. The initial reaction among the rapists' friends and companions, Josh remembers, was revulsion as they identified with the boys. "People heard about it," he tells me, "and they were like, 'Oh, man, those guys are disgusting. How could you, you know, with her? She's retarded.' Nobody really thought it was anything illegal."

Soon the jokes about having sex with a retarded girl were replaced by rumors of a criminal investigation. And then—as Channel 4 broke the story—the school was abuzz with the details of the rape and the first rationalizations. Josh was hearing from his peers that Betty sought and enjoyed the bat and the broomstick. "I don't know if anybody actually believed that," he says, thinking back, "but there were plenty of people who took that line. Especially among girls, actually, girls who were friends with them. There were tons of them, going around saying that this was the type of thing that she wanted to do and enjoyed."

All the kids at Glen Ridge High knew Betty. Although she went to special classes in West Orange, she played on the Glen Ridge basketball and softball teams. "She was famous for...." Josh is trying to make it clear that Betty's overt interest in sex was evident to all the students, and he brings up the incident that the defense lawyers hammered away at during the trial. "She would lift up her shirt, she would make suggestive comments, she would say things to guys."

A reputation as loose and sexually active followed Betty as the investigation progressed, and girls who were friends of the rapists were eager to keep that reputation alive. "Everybody knows how Betty is," Josh remembers the girls telling all comers at school and around town. "She'll do anything, and she wants to do anything."

But Josh does not believe those girls thought the issue through. "The people that defended them and said that she would enjoy this and rationalize it, I think they ignored the fact that it was a baseball bat and a broom. They just kind of said, 'You know how Betty is,' and the baseball bat was never mentioned by people that were their defenders." Josh thinks for a moment about the idea of a bat and broom being an element of consensual sex. "It's really hard to imagine," he says quietly. "All the girls that were saying that she wanted it—none of them would have picked that."

Lace curtains hang over the open window and flutter slightly. The piano in the living room is an old Emerson upright. Family snapshots decorate it. A chess set waits on the piano bench and a book of sheet music is open to the tune "Tomorrow Never Knows." Josh shifts on the couch.

"Whenever you say you're from Glen Ridge, people know where it is now." His chuckle is uncomfortable. "I'm only home during the summers. For the most part people don't talk about it, but it's always there. You can feel that it's always there. Mostly I don't talk about it with people because they'll say things that will make me so angry that I'll know that I won't want to be with them anymore. So in order just to hang out with people, I mostly don't want to talk about it."

Josh adopts this removed attitude when he's home because so many of his neighbors still support the rapists' position that no crime was committed. "They continue to blame the girl somewhat," Josh says, "and they'll say, 'You know how Betty was.'" And Josh keeps quiet about his shock at the slap-on-the-wrist sentence Judge Cohen passed on the guilty. "You have to think it's because they're white suburban kids. I couldn't believe it. I mean, if you were a judge you would think you would be a little more confident in yourself that you could sentence people and not worry that you had made mistakes. If they ever do set foot in this youthful place, they're going to be twenty-eight, thirty years old"—he laughs that short, irritated chuckle again—"in a youthful offender place."

Josh answers questions about the case and about what the rape represents as a symptom of societal degradation without hesitation. He's thought these issues through; they've been on his mind since a few days after the crime became public, when the excitement of TV cameras combing his high school campus lost its luster and the wickedness of the rape became clear to him. "I think that for some reason men everywhere are taught to believe, or believe, that if a woman is inferior to them they have a right to do whatever they want with her sexually. I mean"—he searches for an example and settles on one from current news reports—"in Bosnia. If you think a woman is inferior to you, that's what men seem to think. They seem to think that's what comes with it. Just knowing the way guys at school talk about girls that are less attractive or girls that aren't considered, you know, the top girls, just the attitude they have towards them...." He doesn't finish the sentence but looks over at me expecting that as an American who went through an American high school I know what he means. I ask him to be more specific, to explain that attitude. "Just that they have a right to sexually whatever they want and afterward they have a right to say anything about that person. You know, to call that person a whore or whatever. And especially if someone gets a reputation as a whore, that basically anybody is entitled to her."

But in the next breath, Josh agrees that most men he knows do not subscribe to the misogynistic philosophy he just described, even the men from his insular and sports hero-worshipping high school.

It was the clique surrounding the Scherzers and the Archers that fit the description. "I don't know if it was homosexual or what," he speculates, "but there was definitely something with these guys and sex. They always wanted it to be a display in front of each other. They'd been doing that for years."

Josh stops and clarifies the picture. Members of the gang kept sex with their steady girlfriends a private affair. "But with anyone else, they had been doing it for years; they called themselves voyeurs." He relates the peeping tom story. "They would tell their friends where they were going, and their friends would go up and hide in the closet. Then they would fool around with the girl while their friends were watching. It got around school right away, and I can only imagine how the girls felt when they found out."

Josh knows the stories he retells are true. "I've been at parties where I walked upstairs, and there'd be three guys peering through a door, watching." He's thinking about one party in particular. "The girl was practically passed out, I think, and the guys were whispering in the doorway, 'Move her over this way! Move her over this way!' so that they could get a better look."

■

Josh Golin is not alone in his interpretations. In her study of gang rape committed by university fraternity brothers, *Fraternity Gang Rape*, University of Pennsylvania anthropology professor Peggy Reeves Sanday concludes that "rape is not an integral part of the male nature, but the means by which men programmed for violence and control use sexual aggression to display masculinity and to induct younger men into masculine roles." Like Josh, she sees overtones of homosexuality in activities such as the Glen Ridge rape. "The brothers," she writes about fraternity house gang rapes, "vent their interest in one another through the body of a woman. In the sociodrama that is enacted, the idea that heterosexual males are superior to women and to homosexuals is publicly expressed and probably subjectively absorbed."

Josh interprets the rape of Betty Harris as an obvious outgrowth of the gang's voyeuristic impulses. "I think it was their ultimate thing. I'm sure they would have preferred it if she wasn't retarded. But this way they all got to be out in the open. They got a better view, and they got to all talk to her in front of each other. They got to say dirty things to her in front of each other. They got to see her much better, and they got to tell her to masturbate, and this must have been like...." Josh stops for a moment because he knows he's speculating, but he continues with his theories, theories he's confident are correct. "I mean, I don't know this, but it seems like it was almost an accumulation of everything. This was the big one."

That it was rape, Josh expresses no doubt. But he begins to understand why Betty's mental deficiencies confuse some of his classmates. "A lot of people say, 'They didn't force her, they didn't hold her down and put things in her.' If she wasn't retarded, that's what they would have had to do, and it would have been much more clear-cut. I don't know if it makes it worse that she was retarded. In some ways, it makes people think that it was worse because she's retarded, but, in other ways, it makes people think that it wasn't as bad because they didn't have to force her." He quickly corrects himself: "I mean, they did force her. They didn't have to hold her down, but I don't think when she's home by herself this is the type of thing she does or if she had seen these boys in the park this would have been the type of thing she would have thought to do in front of them. I mean, apparently they said, 'We'll tell your mother if you don't do this thing.' And to her that was the same thing as holding her down."

Josh is just as certain that Betty's retardation was well known to all the rapists and their cronies. "You didn't hear Betty Harris's name said without the word retarded attached to it for years. Everybody knew that."

Just as everybody knew the Scherzers and the Archers and their buddies were the Big Men on Campus. "Feared and respected," Josh recalls with lingering awe and a memory of adolescent respect. "They had always been the big group in school. They got the girls. Maybe that's all it comes down to. They got the girls. The main thing was they were the one group that you couldn't just get in with if you wanted to. I mean if you wanted to get in with the druggies, you did drugs. You could get in with the druggies. If you wanted to get in with the smart people, I mean you can't just be smart, but you could hang out with those kids if that's what you wanted to do. The people in the band, you could hang out with them if that's what you wanted to do. But these guys, they had to pick you to hang out with them. You couldn't just, if you wanted to, you couldn't just say, 'Hey, I'm going to hang out with the Scherzers.' People thought they were jerks, but when you're that age even if you think someone is a jerk, you could still be jealous of them. They acted like they owned the school and they had the girls.

"They certainly talked a lot more about sex and things they had done. But they had done a lot more things than the people I was hanging out with. When I would hear them talk, I would be like, That's wrong to be talking about girls that you fooled around with. That would be part of me. But part of me would also be like, Wow, they did that and they did that." Josh's confused candor is refreshing as he acknowledges, "I mean I don't know what would have happened if me and my friends were, you know, I don't think we would have been like that, but I'm sure in some way we would have, actually."

As Josh thinks back to those days, he vividly remembers the arrogance of the Glen Ridge High sports stars as they paraded through the school day. "They would have this huge lunch table, it was a few tables pushed together, and they'd just be all sprawled out, making a lot of noise. They looked"—he pauses and finds the words—"like they were *it.*" And they still look to some like they are *it*, as they evade punishment for their crime. "I guess by this time they must know how serious and how wrong what they did [was]. But the fact they're free and they may never go to jail or not for a long time when they do, it's going to be a place with cottages and they can get out after six months, that doesn't say what they did, how serious and wrong it was."

∎

Not only was punishment delayed for the criminals by the continued low bail, but society was left unprotected against the possibility of the rapists' striking again while they remained free working on their appeal. Although no formal charges were pressed, there is evidence that at least one of the four Glen Ridge rapists has yet to learn his lesson and, despite Judge Cohen's analysis, is still a danger to society.

While his case dragged through the courts, Christopher Archer went to Boston College to continue his schooling. In October 1990, he went on a date with a girl he met there. Prosecutor Robert Laurino says his research shows that what ensued was what he calls a "rather brutal act." By the time their date ended, says Laurino, Archer "apparently had beaten her severely and sexually assaulted her." After the attack, Laurino says, Archer called himself a "rapist."

This victim signed a sworn affidavit containing her version of the charges, but it wasn't enough to move the judge to keep Archer off the streets. In the written account, the woman is said by Laurino to report that Archer forced her prone, stripped her, and then punched her in the crotch. She never filed a complaint with police, and so there was no official investigation.

Judge Cohen wanted the woman to testify in court, a requirement that Laurino rejected with the explanation, "We would never force a rape victim to come forward. Rape is the most personal crime a woman could ever suffer. It wouldn't be in the interest of rape victims in general and her in particular to produce her." Prosecutors feared that if the woman did testify, her identity, something she did not wish to reveal, would be publicized.

Laurino is concerned Archer and the others present an ongoing threat to society. "Yeah, I think there is that potential there. I think anybody that engages in that nature of barbarous activity—there's always that danger, that threat." He sighs with the resignation that goes with the compromises an Essex County prosecutor must live with day after day. Only $2,500 in bail money was keeping Christopher Archer, the felon Laurino and his colleagues worked so hard to convict, out of prison.

5.

The Trial: The Prosecution Opens

I t took more than three years for the case against the Scherzer twins, Christopher Archer, and Bryant Grober to come before a jury. By the time the trial began, two of the six indicted members of the basement gang had already bargained with the prosecutors to reduce the charges against them. By April 1992, Peter Quigley agreed to perform sixty hours of community service and to testify, if called, once the Glen Ridge case went to trial. In return, charges against him were dropped to a misdemeanor: specifically, endangering the welfare of a mentally incompetent person. As part of the plea bargain, Quigley agreed that he should have left the Scherzers' basement and encouraged others to leave and that he should have tried to stop the rape.

A couple of months later, Paul Archer agreed to a deal with the same terms.

■

After sixteen jurors and alternates were picked on October 14, 1992, to hear the case against the gang, Christopher Archer's lawyer, Thomas Ford, conducted one of his countless impromptu news conferences and summed up the complicated problems the new jury faced. "Consent," said Ford, "is the main issue in the case."

The National Organization for Women attracted attention that day too, as New Jersey chapter president Myra Terry unknowingly took a line from the argument defense lawyer Michael Querques would soon make to the jury. "We're going to stop this 'boys will be boys' attitude from continuing in this country," she announced to a parade of NOW protesters. "This is a pathetic eight-year-old in a woman's body. How could she consent?"

■

Judge Cohen looked up as the jury was brought into his courtroom. "All right, members of the jury," he told them, "we are ready to proceed." He acknowledged assistant prosecutor Glenn Goldberg, who directs Special Prosecutions for Essex County. "Prosecutor," he told Goldberg, "you may make your opening statement on behalf of the State."

After earning a psychology degree and then his law degree at Rutgers, Goldberg briefly practiced law privately, specializing in civil negligence cases, before joining the Essex County Prosecutor's Office back in 1973. He has worked there ever since, assigned, as his curriculum vitae notes, "to prosecute many of Essex County's most complex, difficult, and serious criminal cases, including major public interest cases."

"Thank you, your honor." Goldberg took the courtroom floor. "Counselors," he acknowledged the defense lawyers. "Good morning, members of the jury," he addressed the motley assembly gathered to assess the case he was about to make.

Painstakingly, Goldberg started at Betty Harris's beginning, telling the story of her adoption, her early "different" years, and the diagnosis that something was wrong with the child.

"Neurologically impaired," said Goldberg. "Static encephalopathy —a non-changing organic brain disorder. There was something wrong inside Betty's brain, something about the brain cells. Something wasn't quite right."

The cause was unknown, he told the jurors as he described her short attention span and her intellectual limitations. "By 1983, Betty was eleven and a half years old. Now a child, you know, who is eleven and a half years old is normally in the sixth grade at school, and sixth graders, of course, normally operate at the sixth-grade level and can do sixth-grade work. But," he told the jurors, "you are going to learn that Betty, at age eleven and a half, had finally reached a level of about second or third grade, and from 1983 up until now, Betty has pretty much been frozen in time."

Goldberg told about the special education classes her parents found for their second adopted child and how finally, well after the rape, at the age of twenty-one, just a few months before the trial started, Betty graduated from West Orange High School. "Now when I say graduated, I don't mean to imply that she got an equivalency diploma or came away with the knowledge and education that average, ordinary high school students come away with. Betty Harris reached the age of twenty-one, and she couldn't stay in school any longer—and so she graduated."

As he talked the jurors through Betty's biography, Goldberg annotated her ultimate diagnosis of mentally retarded: "We realize that's not the end of the road. Those words shouldn't have the stigma they may have had in the past, because now we do things for mentally retarded people." He described special classes and the Special Olympics, and he made it a point to explain to the jurors that Betty was able to play the piano by ear and swim strongly and shoot basketball—sports activities that brought her into contact with other children.

"Of course," he pointed out to the jury, "you have to realize that with this mainstreaming and the participating in normal activities with ordinary children, there does arise an increased vulnerability [related] to [being] among people who don't have the same limitations that Betty did, and does."

He identified her tested IQ as in the lowest first or second percentile of the population—telling the jury that before being tested for the trial, year after year, Betty's IQ was measured at under fifty. That level, said Goldberg, placed her in a category called "trainable mentally retarded," technically lower than what is called "educable mentally retarded." It was at this point in his opening argument that

Goldberg made the comparison that followed Betty throughout the trial: At the time of the rape, he said, Betty was "seventeen years old, almost eighteen years old, but at the educational level of an eight-year-old. Betty had the adaptive functioning of an eight-year-old. Her social judgment, her ability to assess social situations, to size them up, to know what is appropriate, what is not appropriate, was that of an eight-year-old."

Further to Goldberg's argument, on May 1, 1991, as he and the other prosecutors worked to get the Glen Ridge rapists to trial, the New Jersey Supreme Court had made a ruling that directly pertained to the crime committed against Betty Harris. The Court defines the limits of the New Jersey law—N.J.S.A. 2C:14-2C(2)—written to punish an act of sexual penetration against a person judged to be mentally deficient compared with the majority of the population. For the purposes of the law, said the court, a person in New Jersey is considered "mentally defective" (the term chosen by the legislature in New Jersey) if, when the sex act occurs, he or she cannot comprehend its sexual nature or—and this clause is crucial to the prosecution of Betty's attackers—he or she is unable to understand the right to refuse to participate in the act or cannot exercise the right to refuse to participate.

Betty, Goldberg told the jurors—and it was one of the crucial points he would need to prove to gain a conviction—is "mentally defective." Goldberg proceeded to explain the legal definition of mentally defective: an IQ below seventy, "a deficiency in adaptive learning, that is to say that she is not on a par with other kids at her age level. She can't adapt, she can't function the way these other children do," and the condition existed before the age of eighteen.

A depressing litany of examples followed, establishing what everyone in Glen Ridge knew, that Betty had always had a learning deficiency. "At age seventeen, when she was going on eighteen, Betty couldn't cook. She couldn't take a recipe and cook something." She could turn on a microwave and pop popcorn, he said, but was unable to handle the complexities of preparing a meal.

"Betty Harris couldn't take public transportation. Betty walked around a lot. She walked around Glen Ridge and did a lot, but she wouldn't be capable of getting on a bus, knowing where to get on, get off, what route to take, couldn't take a train or think about getting on an airplane by herself."

The concept of reconciling change at a store after a transaction was difficult for Betty to negotiate. She could not understand the mechanics of a bank account or engage in a credible job interview. Goldberg said Betty was unable to wash the family dishes alone or even follow the plots of popular television dramas. "What Betty was never able to understand is how could a character be shot and killed one day and be alive again on another day in another TV program, walking around as if nothing had happened."

Goldberg introduced a theme that would be repeated throughout the trial, a description of Betty's personality that adds to the heinousness of the crime the rapists committed against her. The four defendants watched and listened as Goldberg talked about gullibility. "If anybody was nice to Betty at age seventeen, that person was her best friend. To Betty's way of thinking, if somebody showed her a little attention and was nice to her, that person became a good, maybe even her best, friend. Betty Harris at seventeen," he said, "was very naive, very trusting—extremely so."

Goldberg drew the attention of the jurors to Betty's four sullen-looking peers. Because Glen Ridge is such a small town and because all the defendants but Bryant Grober had known her since she was a little girl, all four knew that "she could be easily fooled. She could be easily deceived. She would do almost anything she was told to do, almost anything. She could be easily manipulated, and she could be therefore easily exploited." The prosecutor was building the foundation for the second point that he needed to prove: the four defendants knew that Betty Harris was retarded.

"If one child is different," he reminded the jury, "you know, from your common knowledge, little children talk and children call names and little children can be very cruel sometimes." He stopped for a moment. "So can big children."

It was through Goldberg's opening speech that the jury began to understand Betty—to get to know her. He explained her needs and desires in the context of her deficiencies. "Betty Harris had a very strong need for friendship. Betty Harris needed and wanted friends. Betty Harris did then, as she does now, generally like people. She likes to be around people." Not just any people, but "normal every-day people." And she does not acknowledge her handicap. "Betty Harris does not believe that she is mentally retarded. If you ever were to tell Betty Harris that she is mentally retarded," explained Goldberg, "she wouldn't believe that. She wants to be normal, and she wants to be accepted. She wanted to be accepted in 1989 by her peers, by teenagers that she knew. She wanted to be someone who could go out on dates like normal teenage girls do."

But she wasn't a normal teenager, and she enjoyed no dates. Goldberg laid out her unfortunate life: "In reality, Betty Harris had almost no friends. A lot of acquaintances, but it would be very difficult to categorize most of those people as real friends—let alone good friends. How could Betty Harris go out on a date with an ordinary teenager," Goldberg asked the jurors, "when she couldn't really carry on a normal conversation?"

As an example, Goldberg offered the jurors a glimpse of Betty at school. "The teacher asks a question in class. Betty would raise her hand and say something that really had nothing to do with the subject matter, something that would be inappropriate, and it would annoy people. It would annoy her classmates."

Goldberg told the story of Betty's heading to Carteret Field with her basketball and her portable radio on March 1, 1989. There at the park she encountered her abusers, "boys that she particularly admired. They were the popular boys. They were the football players, the wrestlers, the baseball players, the people that teenagers admired and respected for their physical prowess and abilities, and Betty just thought the most of them. They were, so to speak, her heroes. They were the stars."

Christopher Archer approached Betty with the suggestion that she accompany the group to the Scherzer house. He added the lure of a date with his brother.

"You see," Goldberg outlined for the jury, "Chris Archer had a brother, Paul Archer, a very good-looking, handsome young man, and as much as she liked and admired Chris Archer, Betty really liked his brother. When she was told that Paul Archer would be down there in the basement of the Scherzer house, and she could go down there and meet him, she became interested. Better yet, when she was told that if she came into the Scherzer house and went into the basement, maybe Paul Archer would go out with her—take her out on a date—that was all she needed."

Goldberg drew attention to the premeditated and predatory nature of the encounter orchestrated by Christopher Archer. "So Chris Archer took Betty, led Betty, put his arm around Betty, and guided her a little ways away to the Scherzer house that was right on the edge of this park-like setting. He actually put his arm around Betty and made her feel wonderful. One of these handsome guys that she liked and admired so much was really showing her attention and affection. He had his arm around her in public."

The seductive atmosphere of her removal from the park to the basement was emphasized. "He had his arm around her in public and so she went with Chris Archer to the Scherzer basement. What had been offered to Betty to induce her to go down into the basement was friendship. A date with Paul. Feelings of normalcy. And there was nothing that Betty wanted more than to feel one of them, a part of a normal group of children, young people, friends. Betty Harris thirsted for friends."

Goldberg compared her trip to the basement to the mirage of water for a man dying of thirst in the desert.

"Betty was tricked into the basement," he said. "A carrot was dangled before her, and it was all make-believe. But Betty didn't get it."

Goldberg described the basement, small and packed with about thirteen curious adolescents—all males. He told how Betty was convinced to undress, he described the initial sexual activity between Betty and Bryant Grober, and he drew attention to the boys in the basement who chose to leave the scene. "There was no policeman there to tell them to leave. You see, there are not enough policemen in this world to be in every basement or every situation, but they had the built-in sense and knowledge of what is right and what is wrong, and they were not going to have any part of that—let alone what might happen after that—and they left."

Prosecutors Elizabeth Miller-Hall, Robert Laurino, and Glenn Goldberg wheel a cart with the baseball bat and broom used as evidence during testimony by Betty.

The boys who stayed, Goldberg told the jury, watched and participated as the bizarre basement encounter continued.

"Chris Archer took a broom and put it between Betty's legs—into her vagina," Goldberg explained, pointing out the defendant.

"Stand up, Chris," directed Archer's lawyer, Thomas Ford. "There he is," he told the jury.

"The second man from your right against the wall," Goldberg said, identifying Archer, "who is presently standing, inserted the broom into Betty Harris's body and pushed it in and out and in and out, in and out," he kept repeating, making the sharp contrast between the depravity of the rape and the all-American clean-cut look of Christopher Archer standing in the courtroom.

A Question of Consent

Kevin Scherzer took his turn at the broom, said Goldberg, pushing it "in and out and in and out and in and out for some period of time. This is not something that could have been done or would have been done to—let's say a girlfriend of one of the defendants. This is not something that could have been done or would have been done under these circumstances to any female—quote—ordinary human being." "Ordinary" women, he said, would not "tolerate that type of activity."

Goldberg called the rape aggression, an act of cruelty, humiliation, and degradation—not sex. "When they probed Betty in this way and hurt her—and they did indeed cause her hurt and pain—this was not really what one considers when one thinks about sex." He called it an "obscene science experiment" and a "spectacle," as he described the further assaults with the bat and the stick and specified the exact charges against the four defendants.

■

After a brief break, the jury came back into the courtroom to hear the rest of the prosecutor's opening argument.

Judge Cohen looked over at the jury box. "Members of the jury, first of all, I understand these chairs are a little uncomfortable." He knew it was going to be a long trial. "I will be replacing them. Let me just inquire," he continued his concern, "are any of you jurors uncomfortably warm? If so, just raise your hands. It is slightly warm in the room."

"Stuffy," agreed one of the jurors.

"I don't know if there is much we can do, perhaps we can open one of these windows over here," indicating the narrow slits. "That may alleviate it a little bit. I am feeling a little warm myself." Despite the raw nature of the story Goldberg was telling, the stuffy room was making some people in the courtroom drowsy, and, in fact, as the trial progressed, jurors would often doze through testimony. "Prosecutor, you may continue your opening remarks."

■

Why did they do it?" Goldberg asked. He came up with a long list of possibilities: gratification, arousal, excitement, to make themselves feel important, to show off to each other. Trying to isolate the motive was less important, he told the jurors, than his conclusion that the "reason they did it to Betty is because they could. They knew they could get away with it because they knew some things about Betty Harris. They knew she was loyal. They believed they could rely on her when she promised she would not tell. After all," speculated Goldberg, "suppose she ever did tell anybody. So what? Who would believe Betty Harris, this defective, mentally retarded teenage girl?"

In fact, Betty Harris was so loyal, that when she finally did tell someone what had occurred, it was not to betray her attackers, it was an attempt to prevent another rape. "It was her intent," Goldberg stated, "to protect and to shield the defendants, not to reveal what they had done to her and if she ever had to talk about it, to minimize their crimes—to make them seem less than what they were. You see," he told the jurors, "Betty Harris had a fierce sense of loyalty about her, and a sense of goodness. She was very much afraid of hurting these defendants. Today, Betty Harris regards these four defendants as her good friends. She does not want them to be in any kind of trouble. She does not want anything bad to happen to these defendants that are on trial here today. You will see during the course of this trial that Betty Harris has a good heart. Betty Harris is a good person."

At the time of the crime, Betty already understood the "mechanics of sex," Goldberg acknowledged to the jury. "She knew that sex is putting something in something else." What Betty did not understand that afternoon, he said, was the right to refuse sex. Nor did she know how to refuse a request or demand for sex. "She was unable to say no under the circumstances as they existed in the basement on that day."

Glenn Goldberg was almost finished. "Members of the jury," he said as he concluded his opening summary, "by the time this case is over I submit that each and every one of you will be convinced beyond any doubt whatsoever that these defendants are guilty of these charges. Thank you for your attention."

Goldberg sat down.

■

"If they want to describe it as mechanics of sex," Christopher Archer's lawyer, Thomas Ford, said, ridiculing Goldberg, "she was an expert mechanic." One by one, the four defense lawyers made their counter opening statements.

"All she had to do was say, 'Stop, don't do it.'" Ford simplistically dismissed the implied threats and the coercion suggested by thirteen strong boys surrounding a retarded girl. "That would have been the end of it." He rationalized away the boys' responsibility by insisting that Betty "took the broom into her own hands and inserted it in such a way that didn't injure her in any way." Casting blame on Betty Harris for attempting to reduce any physical trauma as the broom entered her is reminiscent of the argument made in a later Texas case that a rape victim implied consent when she requested that her attacker don a condom. The Texas victim prevailed in court by making it clear that, once she was convinced she could do nothing to prevent the rape, she at least wanted to protect herself from HIV infection.

Michael Querques, Kevin Scherzer's lawyer, introduced his contention that Betty was an experienced seductress, crazed for sex, who loved seeing "the joy on a boy's face when he ejaculated."

From Alan Zegas, lawyer for Bryant Grober, came details about Betty's sexual history and an insistence that the basement encounter was instigated by Betty when she solicited Grober in Carteret Field and "grabbed his crotch."

Louis Esposito, Kyle Scherzer's lawyer, continued to develop the theme that Betty was the responsible party for all that happened to her and that she willingly chose to insert the foreign objects into her vagina, objects that were simply conveniently provided by her classmates.

To bolster its case, the prosecution called on Dr. Susan Esquilin, a psychologist who treats sex abuse victims and who was hired by the state to render an opinion about Betty Harris. She had been used before as an expert witness for the State of New Jersey. Glenn Goldberg had called on her during the high-profile trial of Kelly Michaels, a preschool teacher he prosecuted for the sexual abuse of her students. It was Dr. Esquilin who measured Betty's IQ at sixty-four and assessed her academic and social abilities at the level of an eight-year-old. The psychologist testified that she was convinced from her study of Betty that she was "mentally defective" at the time of the rape.

Prosecutor Robert Laurino led Esquilin through an assessment of Betty's condition. "She's so willing and compliant to do anything anybody asks her," said Esquilin about Betty's behavior in general. Concerning her ability to refuse requests for sex, Esquilin testified, "I don't think she understands that in the sense that she can operate on it. Sexuality for her has much more to do with what somebody asks her to do."

In an attempt to preempt any damage the defense hoped to do when questioning Dr. Esquilin about her interviews with Betty, Laurino provided the opportunity for Esquilin to report that Betty had told her she was sexually experienced: she engaged in sexual relations with boys from Bloomfield, boys offered to pay her for masturbating them, and during junior high school she twice attempted sexual intercourse with Christopher Archer. Betty told the psychologist she had not been forced to commit the acts that occurred in the Scherzer basement, but Esquilin testified that she concluded Betty was coerced because she feared her parents would be told of her sexual activities if she did not cooperate.

During cross-examination, Thomas Ford asked if Betty was obsessed with sex.

"I didn't have any evidence of that," was Esquilin's response. "It was clearly a problem, what happened sexually with other people. I wouldn't call it an obsession."

Ford referred to a conversation during which Betty expressed enjoyment seeing naked boys in a locker room. He asked Esquilin if such a quote suggested "intensive interest" in sex.

"The passage would indicate an interest," was the response. It was quickly followed by the obvious: "People have an interest in sex. She's interested in looking."

Then came a most important question. Ford asked Dr. Esquilin if Betty understood that she had the right to say no to sex.

She understands the meaning of *no,* answered Esquilin, but "I don't think she understands how that operates at all. As soon as she gets into a social encounter and someone wants her to do something, I don't think she has any capacity to say no."

In addition to proving that Betty was unable to say no, the State needed to prove that the rapists were aware of her inability. Ford asked Dr. Esquilin what her appraisal of Betty would have been absent the formal testing that resulted in the measurement of a sixty-four IQ.

"Anyone who spent more than a few minutes" with Betty, said Esquilin, joining the refrain heard throughout the trial, would recognize in her a mentality that was "different, wrong, peculiar, and lacking."

Michael Querques used his opportunity to question Esquilin as a platform to make the jury aware of Betty's sexual past. He asked if Esquilin was aware of various sexual escapades he charged Betty with experiencing. Some the psychologist knew about, others she didn't. But the jury heard about all of them. Finally Querques asked her if her research showed that the retarded do not control their sexual urges well. "Some do," answered Esquilin, "some don't."

Querques made two valiant attempts during his cross-examination of Esquilin to debunk the prosecution claim that Betty was unable to say no. He read to her from a state psychiatric report in which Betty was asked if she would again participate in the activities that occurred during the rape. "I probably would say no, but I'd do it for the money," was her reply. Querques asked Esquilin if that answer shows Betty can say no to sex. "That's what it says," acknowledged Esquilin.

Next Querques read from Betty's grand jury testimony. "I didn't do Kyle," Betty told the grand jury, "because I didn't want to." Again, he suggested, the remark showed she could make sexual choices, could say no. Dr. Esquilin rejected his contention. Her diagnosis resulted in the conclusion that Betty "has no understanding of the consent issues."

■

"I assume she became more and more bewildered. She did not comprehend the right to refuse. She didn't grasp she could refuse to participate," testified Dr. Gerald Meyerhoff. Former chief of psychiatry at Bergen Pines County Hospital in Paramus, New Jersey, Dr. Meyerhoff was hired by the prosecution as an expert witness. He studied Betty Harris during three hours of interviews before arriving at his conclusions, and his work included meetings with Betty's parents and sister, her teachers and coaches.

Betty is mentally defective, Dr. Meyerhoff concluded for the court without hesitation. The fact that she remained in the Scherzer basement throughout her ordeal—that she did not run or yell or try to escape or complain—proves, he testified, what she later made clear herself with her cry for help to her swimming coach. She did not know how to say no. Her inability to understand her right to refuse sex, and her inability to comprehend how to prevent unwanted sex from occurring, were compounded as problems that afternoon, Dr. Meyerhoff told the jurors, by her lust for friendship.

"This is an important piece of her life," the psychiatrist testified, "her search for friends." During their session together, Meyerhoff said Betty explained, "I let them do it. I didn't want to lose them. They wouldn't brag. They knew I was a nice girl who wouldn't tell on them. They really do like me and love me and think I'm special. I don't understand why they like me and take me down to the basement when they always call me retarded." Meyerhoff said Betty's confused questioning of the boys' motivation for taking her down to the basement is the only indication he was able to elicit from her that she even remotely comprehended she was a victim that afternoon.

"She did not fully understand being used," he testified, and said that when he asked Betty if she enjoyed sex, "she didn't seem to understand. I had a feeling she was quite asexual. It was an activity without gratification or great joy."

The defense tried to mock Dr. Meyerhoff's credibility by drawing attention to his high expert witness fees—as much as two hundred dollars an hour for a total of almost twenty thousand dollars. Louis Esposito dismissed the psychiatrist as a "pompous, pretentious windbag." During his summation at the end of the trial, Esposito tried to convince the jury that Dr. Meyerhoff's diagnosis that Betty was mentally defective was tainted by the money he received, as were Dr. Esquilin's professional results. "Their opinions, I submit," he announced to the jurors, "had been purchased."

Instead, Esposito wanted jurors to remember that during Betty's troubled school days, her parents received conflicting reports about their daughter's mental abilities—proof, he claimed, that even experts employed by the Essex County public schools "didn't know and still don't know the exact diagnosis." Esposito tried to use this fact to show that the rapists did not necessarily know Betty was retarded when they took her to the basement. "My client," he insisted as he ran through the litany of diagnoses offered over the years to explain Betty's deficiencies, "is in no better position than any of these people."

■

For its final argument, before the defense lawyers rose to present their side of the case, the prosecution used television monitors in the courtroom to project drawings Betty made several months after the attack, drawings that depict the rape. The jurors looked at Betty's shocking, simple stick figures of herself in the basement: performing fellatio, lying prone on the couch suffering the broom, bat, and stick.

Psychiatric nurse and University of Pennsylvania professor Ann Burgess assigned Betty to make the drawings during the interview she conducted in October 1989. Back in 1974, Dr. Burgess and a colleague developed the concept of rape trauma syndrome, a diagnosis that is used to help explain both why rape victims often delay reporting the crime and why their descriptions of the rape sometimes differ as police investigations proceed. She interpreted the dark scratches Betty made around the sex acts in the pictures as evidence that Betty was upset about the events she drew. Her testimony marked the first time a New Jersey judge allowed testimony about rape trauma syndrome to be introduced as trial evidence. After the rapists were convicted, their lawyers announced that their appeal of the guilty verdict would be based partly on disputing the veracity of Dr. Burgess's theories and testimony.

6

Querques's Lolita Defense

C all Michael Querques to query him about his botched defense of Kevin Scherzer, and the hardened Jersey lawyer—his long resume includes trial work for clients convicted of involvement with organized crime—slams the phone down to break the connection. His reticence to discuss what became infamous as his "Lolita defense" is understandable. Not only did Querques lose the case; he lost it with the bizarre and invidious argument that Betty not only enjoyed the rape, she instigated it.

Betty Harris enjoyed seeing "the joy on a boy's face when he ejaculated," he told the jury as the defense began its arguments. "She thrived for affection," he said, "but she also thrived for the kissing, she craved the caressing, she craved the embracing, she craved the euphoria because her brain functioned in that way. You may very well find," he suggested to the jury, "in the condition she had, her feeling for sex and her drive, her genitals' signals, are greater than normal."

Making a fool of himself in front of a jury is no new experience for Michael Querques. In the mid-eighties he worked for Francesco "Frank" Polizzi, a defendant in the so-called Pizza Connection case, a case the government identified as one of its most important drug and Mafia cases ever to come to trial. He is "small and intense,"

Shana Alexander writes of Querques in her book about the case, "with white skin, black glasses, delicate features."

Querques lost the Pizza Connection case; among his adversaries on the prosecution side of that courtroom was Louis Freeh, destined to be appointed director of the Federal Bureau of Investigation by President Clinton. In *The Pizza Connection,* author Alexander recounts the moment in court when Querques tried to convince the jury that a bag passed to Polizzi was full of sardines, not Mafia cash:

> Querques asks Mrs. Polizzi to display the contents of her paper bag to the court and the jury. She holds up two ice packs and two pounds of half-frozen smelts, explaining that fresh sardines are out of season. With great flourish Querques produces another paper bag, folded and stapled—the same one jurors, months ago, watched the agent fold to resemble the bag he saw Salamone hand to Polizzi in the dark parking lot.
>
> Querques asks Mrs. Polizzi to transfer the fish from her bag to this one, so the jury can see that this one is big enough to contain two pounds of fish, with ice packs. The whole thing is pure theatrics—and theater turns to accidental hilarious farce when Cecolia Polizzi picks up her bag. The melting ice packs have soaked the papers through, and the fishy cargo drops out of the soggy bottom, splashing brine in all directions and destroying Polizzi's entire case. The prosecution need not even argue that a grocery bag that contained fish and ice could not have remained intact on a three-hour drive on a June night. The defense had just dramatically proved the point.

Querques's theatrics again proved farcical in the midst of the Glen Ridge case, when he tried to paint Betty Harris not as a victim, but as responsible for the crime that was committed against her. "All girls are not the same. There are some girls who are Lolitas," Querques proclaimed to the jury in one of his most infamous arguments during the trial. He asked them rhetorically, "Do you know Lolitas, fourteen, fifteen, and dress up like they are eighteen and nineteen, to entice and attract?"

This comparison of Betty with Vladimir Nabokov's fictional character is not just offensive, it is inaccurate. Lolita was not attacked by a band of classmates preying on her inability to say no. Lolita was not abused with a broomstick, a bat, and a dirty stick. Lolita's intelligence quotient was measured at 121, not sixty-four. And perhaps the most important point Querques overlooked when he dragged Lolita into the trial is that from the beginning of Nabokov's novel, Humbert Humbert acknowledges that he is a criminal—despite the fact that it is Lolita, there in Room 342 of The Enchanted Hunter, who finally says to Humbert, "Okay, here is where we start."

■

"Are you ready to proceed?" Judge Cohen asked Michael Querques as the defense began its responses to the rape charges detailed by the state.

Christopher Archer's lawyer, Thomas Ford, had already fed the jury details of Betty's sexual experiences prior to the rape. Bryant Grober's advocate, Alan Zegas, had done the same. Louis Esposito, Kyle Scherzer's representative, would follow up Querques's opening message by insisting that Betty willingly not only took off her clothes but also voluntarily inserted the broom into herself and sought help with the baseball bat because she could not maneuver it unassisted.

"Ready," Querques responded to the judge.

"Please bring the jury out," ordered Judge Cohen.

With the jury back in courtroom, Judge Cohen continued the trial. "Members of the jury," he told them with his usual calm voice and inscrutable face, "we are ready to continue. We will hear next an opening statement from Mr. Michael Querques on behalf of his client, Kevin Scherzer."

Querques took the floor and began his Lolita defense. He started with a tortured retelling of Abraham Lincoln's adage that you cannot fool all of the people all of the time. "Now I am no Abe Lincoln," Querques said in the first of several self-deprecating observations. "I am just fortunate that I know what he said, and I am fortunate that I believe what he said."

After a convoluted testimonial to "human decency, honesty, truth, character, and integrity," Querques called his client from the defense table. "Mr. Scherzer," he said. "Come here a minute. Come here."

When Kevin Scherzer stood up, Querques told the jury, "Take a good look. Take a long look." Throughout the trial all the defendants appeared hard, athletic, well-dressed, in control. "Come closer, Kevin," coaxed Querques. "They have been seeing you from afar."

Again addressing the jury, Querques said, "You know what you see, because he is up close, what you see is who I have been calling a young man, and he is that. But you are not going to judge a young man, now age twenty-one. You are going to judge a teenager of eighteen."

Querques was setting up his fiction that the rape was merely a childhood lark. "Fairness dictates," he instructed the jury, "you turn back the clock to March 1, 1989, which I make out to be exactly three years and seven and a half months ago. That's what we're going to talk about, not today."

"I brought him up here," he said of his client, "because yesterday I heard Mr. Goldberg tell you that he, Kevin Scherzer, is a heinous, venomous person, that he is guilty of first-degree crimes, which is a bunch of crimes that are exceeded only by murder. That's what he told you.

"And when he talked about conspiracy, he said that this then-teenager plotted, conspired, collaborated with others to rape, and did in fact rape, one Betty Harris."

Querques told the jury he would prove that no rape took place because "life is different than theory. Life has advantages and disadvantages," he said, alluding to Scherzer's athletic successes and popularity and Betty Harris's retardation. "It has kindnesses, and it has ugliness; it has beauty, it has distortion."

Next came another instruction to the jury. "You are not going," he told them, "to leave your common sense at home. You are not going to leave your experience at home."

It was at this point that Querques started to head into the disastrous "boys will be boys" argument and the defense contention that

Betty incited her own rape. "The women will have to dig in," Querques told the women on the jury, "and ask yourselves what it was like to be seventeen and a female in 1989. You will also be asked to think, though you are females, about what a youngster of eighteen or seventeen or sixteen goes through, how he functions, what he thinks, what he does." He said it again: "What he does."

And, as if all New Jersey adolescents hang out in basements probing their retarded classmates with bats and brooms, he added, "If you are fair, you will not hold anybody to a higher degree of judgment and experience than you." Again referring to prosecutor Goldberg's charges, Querques steamed ahead: "We are going to prove to you that which he says transpired never transpired." At this point Querques made a technical correction, because the defense never denied the basic prosecution contention that Betty was violated with the bat and the stick and the broom. "Certainly never transpired with that evil purpose," Querques corrected, "and that corrupt, venomous intention, to hurt this young lady, or to take advantage of this young lady."

On the contrary, claimed Querques, Betty was "ready, willing, and able to do what she did. Besides being ready, willing, and able, she was anxious to do what she did."

■

Somewhere, sometimes there may be women who are ready, willing, and anxious for a group of men to jam broomsticks, bats, and dirty dowels into them. The jury in the Glen Ridge case decided that Betty Harris was not ready, willing, and anxious to be on the receiving end of Kevin Scherzer's perverse assault in his parents' basement.

In her thorough study of rape, *Against Our Will: Men, Women and Rape*, a book that was instrumental in raising awareness of rape, author Susan Brownmiller found that "the ramming of a stick, a bottle or some other object into a woman's vagina is not an uncommon *coup de grâce*" during rapes. Searching through the histories of wars, Brownmiller found the sexual abuse of women with some sort of object to be a recurring crime.

For example, at the 1946 International Military Tribunal for the Far East in Tokyo, testimony about the abuses of the Japanese army in Nanking included several stories of rapes culminating with a stick inserted in the victim's vagina.

Other examples Brownmiller found came from the 1971 Winter Soldier Investigation: An Inquiry into American War Crimes, a meeting called by the Vietnam Veterans Against the War organization. A sergeant named Scott Camil, who served with the First Battalion, Eleventh Marine Regiment, First Marine Division in 1966 and 1967 told his colleagues about arriving in a village where a Vietnamese woman had been shot by an American sniper.

"When we got up to her she was asking for water. And the lieutenant said to kill her. So he ripped off her clothes, they stabbed her in both breasts, they spread her eagle and shoved an E tool up her vagina, an entrenching tool, and she was still asking for water. And then they took that out and they used a tree limb and then she was shot."

At the same veterans' meeting, John Mallory, a civic action officer attached in 1969 and 1970 to the First Squadron, eleventh Armored Cavalry Regiment, First Air Cavalry Division shared a similar story. "On one occasion," he recalled, "a North Vietnamese Army nurse was killed by the 11th Armored Cavalry troops; subsequently a grease gun of the type used in automotive work was placed in her vagina and she was packed full of grease."

Not all incidents of sticks and other foreign objects being forced into women occur during wartime. The Boston Strangler killed, raped, and then left his victims with a broomstick or a wine bottle stuffed up their vaginas. "I think it's just generally a matter of convenience," theorizes Robert Laurino about the frequent appearance of brooms in foreign object rape. "It's there. They grab whatever implement is there."

For the comprehensive study *Rape in America*, scientists working with the National Victims Center in Washington and the Crime Victims Research and Treatment Center at the Medical University of South Carolina tracked over four thousand American women nationwide. Although the incidence of foreign object rape is minimal compared with the overall number of rapes in America, the study concludes that such assaults are a distinct and real element of violent and unwanted sexual attacks on women. Such attacks occur with enough frequency that some police jurisdictions include, on the forms that their officers use to collect information about reported rapes, a specific space for a description of the types of foreign objects used by rapists.

In most literature the assaulted women are not "ready, willing, and anxious" either. The graphic gang rape of Tralala in *Last Exit to Brooklyn* begins with her drunken offer to service sexually everyone in a bar. It ends as rape. Author Hubert Selby describes "the kids who were watching and waiting to take a turn took out their disappointment on Tralala and tore her clothes to small scraps put out a few cigarettes on her nipples pissed on her jerkedoff on her jammed a broomstick up her snatch then bored left her lying amongst the broken bottles rusty cans and rubble...."

Although the wrong man was found guilty by the Mississippi jury, foreign object rape was integral to the case presented by William Faulkner in *Sanctuary*. In the story, Faulkner's violent character Popeye used a corn-cob in response to his sexual dysfunction when he raped Temple. After the secret was revealed in court, it was, of course, the talk of the town:

> The drummers sat a little while longer along the curb before the hotel, Horace among them; the south-bound train ran at one oclock. 'They're going to let him get a way with it, are they?" a drummer said. "With that corncob? What kind of folks have you got here? What does it take to make you folks mad?"
>
> "He wouldn't a never got a trial, in my town," a second said.
>
> "To jail, even," a third said.

What is missing from history and literature is the suggestion that many women are "ready, willing, and anxious" to be on the receiving end of such abuse. Even calls I made to the providers of a wide range of sexual services who advertise in the back pages of

America's sexually explicit tabloid newspapers failed to locate a sub-culture where broomsticks and baseball bats play a role in consensual sex. Nonetheless, somewhere, someone—and probably more than one—chooses bats and brooms as their implement of choice for sexual penetration.

In his *Studies in the Psychology of Sex*, the maverick self-taught sex expert Havelock Ellis traces the long history of dildos back to the dawn of civilization. "The use of an artificial penis in solitary sexual gratification may be traced down from classic times," he writes, "and doubtless prevailed in the very earliest human civilizations." He reports a long list of foreign objects to have been found in vaginas or bladders and required surgical intervention for removal. "Pencils, sticks of sealing wax, cotton-reels, hair-pins, bodkins, knitting needles, crochet-needles, compasses, glass stoppers, candles, corks, tumblers, forks, tooth-picks, tooth-brushes" are all on his list, as is "a full-sized hen's egg removed from the vagina of a middle-aged woman."

Naturally not all the items Ellis found used as dildos caused medical problems. "The banana seems to be widely used for masturbation by women," writes Ellis, who cites a poem he found in the *Arabian Nights*: "O bananas, of soft and smooth skins, which dilate the eyes of young girls. You, alone among fruits are endowed with a pitying heart, O consolers of widows and divorced women." Cucumbers, carrots, and turnips are also in Ellis's inventory of foreign objects used by choice.

Writer Laura Miller specializes in keeping current with trends in sexuality. "You name it," she sums up the world of sexual behavior, "and there's somebody somewhere who likes doing it." Miller reviews pornographic videotapes for *Future Sex* magazine. Based on her own journalistic studies, she told me she too rejects Querques's argument that the bat and broom and stick were Betty's idea of fun: "Women don't use sex toys with men present."

Susie Bright keeps a dowel stick dildo in her own sex toy box and agrees that most women do not use foreign objects for sexual gratification when they are interacting with sex partners. One reason is shyness, a societal inhibition against such public behavior. Another more practical explanation she offers is that the woman knows how much pressure to exert to ensure that she brings herself pleasure and not pain. "It's much easier to do that kind of thing to yourself, to penetrate yourself and control everything about it. You know whether it feels good or doesn't feel good. You control the motion completely yourself," says Bright, a flamboyant sex educator who lectures and writes using material collected from her vast personal experiences on the frontiers of American's sex culture.

When we talked about sex and the Glen Ridge case, she stressed her firm belief that pornography does not cause crimes such as the Glen Ridge rape and probably did not serve as an instruction manual for it. Bright pointed out how difficult she thinks it would be for kids in Glen Ridge to get their hands on many films specifically depicting rape with a foreign object, explaining that after the Meese Commission report on pornography prepared by the Justice Department during the Reagan administration was issued, most commercial pornographers ceased producing movies starring broomsticks, bats, and other such implements. The report singled out rape pictures as particularly damaging and dangerous. Prosecutors around the country then brought charges frequently and successfully against purveyors of rape films. Moviemakers responded by moving on to other, less legally risky themes. "If they did watch anything like that," she told me about the Glen Ridge boys, "it would either be made by amateurs, or very old." Broom handles and bats are not usually used in pornographic films no matter how aggressive law enforcement acts, says Bright. "Even in the salad days of porn, when directors felt more like they could treat issues like violence, I never saw anything like a broom handle. That imagery is not out of hard-core pornography, where you use major hardware to terrorize women. Slasher films and horror films are very big on using imposing phallic symbols to frighten women."

At the time the Meese Commission report was released, Patrick Trueman was chief of the child exploitation and obscenity section of the criminal division of the Justice Department. He agrees with Bright that the report eradicated production of most rape films. "The harder films were sure winners, an easy conviction," he told me about his experiences working with prosecutors after the report was completed. "None of the porn companies are producing rape films anymore," he says. But he is convinced plenty are still left on store shelves. "You could go into Manhattan today and get them," he says about movies depicting rape, foreign object or otherwise.

It is common, Bright asserts along with Havelock Ellis, for girls and women to insert foreign objects into their vaginas—both as experimentation and for sexual pleasure. "Young girls have a propensity for sticking things into themselves," she says, remembering her own foreign object initiation with a chemist's pestle. The use of household objects for vaginal self-penetration is normal and to be expected, she says, easily making up a long list of items she is familiar with for their use as dildos: hairbrush handles, shampoo bottles, wooden spoons, zucchinis, and carrots. "Anything insertable, anything that looks like it's smooth is attractive," she says, adding candles and flashlights.

But, despite the extensive catalog of homemade and makeshift dildos used through the ages, brooms and bats are rarely a foreign object of choice for women. They can present problems when being manipulated alone because they are so long, and they simply are not practical for consensual sex. "They are unwieldy because of the length of them," explains Bright, "and it's kind of heavy and awkward. Why not use something shorter? And because you're not going to be able to penetrate someone fully with that, there's a lot of distance. Usually when you're fucking someone with a dildo, even if it's a really big one, you're still really close to the person. For masturbation, it's too unwieldy, and between two lovers who use objects for penetration, it would also be unwieldy. It's just more convenient to use something smaller."

For Susie Bright, the issue is not whether Betty Harris might wish to be masturbated with a bat and a broom; the issue is simply consent.

When I asked Leslie Walker-Hirsch, a psychologist who specializes in the sexuality of retarded people, if she ever encountered women, retarded or otherwise, who identified penetration with bats and brooms as an activity of choice, her answer was a simple and direct, "Never."

Eighteen years after *Against Our Will* was first published, I talked with Susan Brownmiller about her research into foreign object rape. "I think it goes with urination and defecation and splashing of semen," she theorized, as another manner of degrading a victim. She still has not encountered any definitive study of the phenomenon, but Brownmiller long ago concluded that dildo desire in general is, as she put it, "part of the male mythology. It gets perpetuated in pornography," she said. "It certainly is in the erotic literature of lesbianism, but most of that has been written by men."

She followed the Glen Ridge case in the papers, spent a day in the courtroom during the trial, and was shocked by Querques's "ready, willing, and anxious" claim. "It was astonishing in this day and age," she said. "Obviously they can still argue it and maybe believe it. But it's part of the myth: The harder you push the more she's supposed to respond."

■

Nonetheless, lawyer Michael Querques was insistent with his arguments. "When you think about March 1, 1989," he told the jury, "you have to put yourselves back as best you can into what happened that day, how it happened, why it happened.

"Maybe I can sum it up in a few words," he suggested, "and put it to you this way. What is the chemistry? What is the chemistry that caused this to happen?

"Young Betty Harris like many, many girls, if not all girls—and it doesn't matter to me if you say all girls, it doesn't matter—Betty Harris was trained, educated, taught at home, taught in school, perhaps, that sex is to be engaged in only when there is a mutual relationship of love, that you have sex when you are married, that you have sex to bear children. It is not a fun thing. It is not something you play with.

"The difficulty," he went on, "is that most people, I believe most people, and I am certain that the testimony will show that when it comes to Betty Harris, Betty Harris like many people, discovered that it is pleasurable to give sex, to see the joy on a boy's face when he ejaculates, or to use her word, comes.

"She learned it was pleasurable to have sex given to her, when it comes to pleasure that the giving and the receiving of sex simultaneously is wonderful. She on her own perhaps learned other things, as well, as to the pleasure of sex. She learned before 1989 that in this country, but particularly in this country, you are born a free woman, and that when you are born a free woman you have choices that are yours."

Querques hurtled on, taking full advantage of the holes the judges allowed in the rape shield law, legislation designed to protect the privacy of rape victims.

"You make choices as to what direction your life goes in," Querques said. "Just like one kid is dedicated to becoming a doctor, another one wants to be a fireman, and on and on and on. When it comes to your behavior, you likewise have choices. You can pick your friends. You can pick your sports. You can pick your fantasies. You can pick your movies. You can pick anything. The choices were hers, and she knew it just like you know it. Her retardation aside." But her retardation could not be cast aside, Querques eventually learned. It was crucial to the case against his client.

Next came rhetorical questions, again an attempt to blur the clear difference between consensual and nonconsensual activities. "Did this young lady know what it felt like to touch skin, to caress it, the opposite sex's body? Did she know what it was to kiss and the pleasure that comes from kissing?"

Querques talked to the jury about instinct, hunger, and thirst. "What about sex? Is it any different? Do I come from another planet? Or is sex something you get a message about?" Here Querques started to lay the groundwork for another bizarre aspect of his defense. He blamed not just Betty for the attack, but also Betty's parents. "If you are a father and a mother, do you get concerned about having a young boy finding out the bed is wet, not because he is three years old, he isn't trained yet—because he had a wet dream?"

"What is going on?" his prattle continued. "Mother Nature is at work. That's what is going on, and Mother Nature is the good Lord. What, did we all forget that? You don't want to think about that? You think that's an ugly subject? You don't think that's a part of life? You don't think that's what went on in this case? Or do you think Betty Harris, because she is retarded, doesn't have feelings?"

Querques came right back with his answers.

"She's got them." And he had more bizarre surprises for the jury as he diagnosed Betty. "Let me tell you, you may very well find out that in that condition she had her feelings for sex, her drive, if you like, for sex. Her brain and her stomach and her genital signals are greater than normal. Obsession. One word. Obsession. Some people have the obsession. Some people eat themselves into oblivion because they love food, some people want to have sex, I never understood it, morning, noon, and night. I don't know whether they are lucky or unlucky, but that's not the problem here. The problem is, whether or not she liked it, she certainly understood it."

Querques then told the jury about Betty's birth control pill prescription, written by her doctor over a year before the attack in the Scherzers' basement. In the doctor's records, Querques reported, was a statement from Betty's mother that the pills were needed because Betty was sexually active.

"If that doesn't prove that the mother was on notice that [Betty] was engaging in sex, I don't know what does. If that doesn't prove she did something to protect her daughter from becoming pregnant, I don't know what does."

Next he was pursuing the victim again, based not on what happened in the basement, but on the history of her sex life. "I want to scream these words out," Querques worked the jury. "She knows what sex is. She knows what to do. The truth is she knows what to do better perhaps than old-fashioned adults like me, because there is one big difference between the 1940s and the 1980s; what was considered perversion in 1940 is not considered perversion at all today by most people." Maybe at that point Querques realized most people still list assaults with brooms, bats, and sticks as perverse. He changed his wording. "Or at least some people, and since we have choices you can engage in what some call perversion and others say beauty, wonderful. It's glorious. It's euphoric. It's ecstatic."

With that flourish, Querques began his case for blaming his client's crime not just on Betty Harris, her retardation, and her mother—he added modern American society.

■

As is the case in forty-seven of the United States, New Jersey law includes a rape shield statute. N.J.S.A. 2C:14-7 is designed to protect victims in rape cases. The idea is that a victim's sexual history should not be flagrantly available for public consumption during a rape trial and, of much more vital concern, a victim's past sexual experiences should have no bearing on determining if a rape occurred.

However, N.J.S.A. 2C:14-7 allows for some exceptions. The law provides judges with the latitude to puncture the shield if they find the rights of the victim's privacy in conflict with the fair trial rights of defendants.

Before Betty Harris's case went to trial, another New Jersey judge was assigned to preside over pretrial hearings held to determine if Betty would enjoy the protections potentially extended by the rape shield law. "Confidentiality and privilege must give way when they conflict with rights to a fair trial," was the conclusion of Judge Burrell Ives Humphreys as he ruled that scenes from Betty's past sex life could be presented to the jury. In his ruling, the judge acknowledged the pain such a public discussion of her private life might cause Betty. Critical to Judge Humphrey's ruling was the prosecution's argument that Betty's retardation denied her the ability to refuse to participate in the basement activities that led to the rape charges. He decided that the rights of the defendants included the opportunity to use some evidence of Betty's sexual past to try to prove that she functioned well enough to make sexual choices. "There is no fair alternative to a vigorous and searching quest for the truth," was the explanation he gave for his decision. "From truth springs justice," he continued. "To shroud the truth is to invite an unjust verdict."

The defense was limited to discussing only those sexual activities of Betty's that were relevant to the case and was specifically restricted by N.J.S.A. 2C:14-7, which states, "Evidence of previous sexual conduct shall not be considered relevant unless it is material to negating the element of force or coercion or to proving that the source of semen, pregnancy or disease is a person other than the defendant."

Trial Judge Cohen held hearings in his chambers to decide exactly what evidence dealing with Betty's sex life could be presented by the defense. The arguments and conclusions were sealed from the public in an attempt to protect Betty's little remaining privacy. As part of the difficult balancing act the judge was obligated to perform, he allowed the defense access to Betty's gynecological records, despite the fact that the release of those records violated patient-doctor confidentiality.

"We have no problems with the judge's ruling," prosecutor Glenn Goldberg said after the hearing. Throughout the trial, the prosecutors contended that Betty's promiscuity only reinforced their claim that she did not know how to say no.

At one point during the trial, Judge Cohen dropped his usual reserve and charged the defense with taking advantage of the openings he and Judge Humphreys offered them and with trying to "completely eviscerate" the rape shield law. The judge's outburst was triggered during the questioning of one of the defendants' friends. James Bolen was part of the original crowd gathered before the rape in the Scherzers' basement. He testified that he left the scene as Betty approached Bryant Grober, Grober's pants down around his knees. Bolen was an eyewitness to the crime for the prosecution, and he was not asked why he left the basement. When, during cross-examination, defense lawyer Thomas Ford did ask him why, the prosecution objected, and the judge dismissed the jury for a lunch break.

It was during that break that the judge lost his temper at the defense lawyers, telling them that he would not allow the question to be answered. If permitted to answer, Bolen likely would have told the jury that he left the basement because he expected Betty, based on what he had heard about her reputation, to engage in some sort of sexual activity that he did not wish to see. The defense had not cleared the question with the judge during the pretrial hearings dealing with rape shield law restrictions. Michael Querques argued with the judge, insisting that even if Bolen's answer would violate the intent of the shield law, "it has to yield to the right of a fair trial."

Judge Cohen was angry as he ruled that Bolen's response would be hearsay, not evidence—Bolen would be talking about Betty Harris's reputation, not activities he personally experienced or witnessed. Attempting to depict Betty for the jury as "some kind of loose woman who consented to sexual acts in the past and therefore probably consented this time" would not be allowed, the judge insisted, calling the line of questioning directed at James Bolen an attempt to elicit "highly prejudicial and highly inflammatory" comments about Betty and aspects of her past sex life completely unrelated to the rape. "You've been trying to do that since day one," Judge Cohen preached to the defense lawyers, "and I'm not going to permit it. I'm not going to permit you to do an end run on the rape shield rules."

"It can never be absolute," prosecutor Robert Laurino acknowledged about the rape shield law after the trial was over. "You're always going to have that tension of the rights of the defendant versus the rights of the victim. There was this balancing by Judge Cohen," he complimented the judge. "Roughly speaking, maybe 25 percent of the materials were not let in," he says about information pertaining to Betty's sexual history that the jury never learned. "Not as much as we would have liked."

■

"Understandings," said Querques to the jury as his belabored and embarrassing argument continued. "It's not easy, is it? You can make it easy by giving people the benefit of, the opportunity to do in life what they like to do and without setting yourself up as some special person who will say I don't like what she did, I don't like what he did. It's wrong."

Lawyer Querques was quick to explain that he understood. "I am going to condemn them," he said about the events in the basement. "I am going to condemn him," he said about Kevin Scherzer and his participation in those events. "I am going to condemn her,"— that he'd already made abundantly clear—"It's wrong by any moral standards."

Then he was back after Betty Harris. "Betty Harris was first of all attracted to boys, particularly cute boys. That's her word. 'Is he cute?' 'Oh, yeah, he is cute.' 'Oh, gee, I met him, he is cute.'

"She had, for a seventeen-year-old, as I have already said, knowledge, a vast knowledge of having sex, doing sex, and what sex was all about. Don't be offended," he warned the jury. "She uses the word 'penis'. As synonymous for penis she will use 'dick,' she will use 'prick,' she will use 'boner.' For fellatio she will say 'blow job.' For orgasm she will say 'come.'

"Besides being attracted to boys and having knowledge of sex, she had an aggression. She had an aggressive attitude toward sex." Querques then reiterated the story told earlier by one of the other defense lawyers that the day of the assault Betty had put her hand between Bryant Grober's legs.

"There were many other instances," said Querques, again taking advantage of the penetrated rape shield law. "At Columbia High School in the music class, taking her shirt and exposing her breasts in this manner, by lifting her shirt to the extent that the music teacher almost had a heart attack.

"She had and still has emotional and physical needs. One of those was, Mr. Goldberg put his finger on it yesterday, she wanted affection, she thrived for affection. That is an absolute given. But she also thrived for the kissing, she craved the caressing, she craved the embracing, she craved that euphoria, that ecstasy in a simple word, the pleasure of engaging in sex, because her brain functioned that way."

Querques was veering out of control. "She is a full-breasted young lady," he added inexplicably. "She is a full-blown young lady—was at fifteen, sixteen, seventeen—and if you are going to have sympathy, have sympathy for someone who needs and someone who desires sex in the same way that you have feelings and sympathy and understanding for a person dying of hunger. Hunger … is really no different, is it? Because it is the human system that craves food, drink, affection, love, pleasure, and s-e-x.

"She had those needs just like you and me and no matter how she tests on an IQ test, she has those same needs, and she is going to do like you and me. When the trigger goes off, when the feeling goes off, if you have got a lady friend you do it, if you have a wife you do it, it is not pleasant to talk this way, but it is necessary."

Perhaps Querques felt at this point that his speech was counterproductive because as he continued he said, "Let's talk about another thing. I am going to tell you something, I run a risk. Maybe I have run other risks this morning, but this is a known risk, this is a risk I take knowing I am taking a risk."

He acknowledged the women on the jury and instructed them about his Lolita theory. "Girls will be girls. All girls are not the same. There are some girls who are Lolitas. Do you know Lolitas, fourteen, fifteen, and dress up like they are eighteen and nineteen, to entice and attract?"

Querques noted that his analysis came from personal experience. "I have a daughter, a big-breasted girl, walks this way to hide her breasts. Her sister is flat, she sticks it out, what little she has got, so I know what I am talking about. You come in all shapes and sizes," he explained to the women jurors. "You come in all desires. You come from all kinds of backgrounds, and you all have your own values and then you also have what Mother Nature put inside you, and there are some that are very, very flirtatious."

Querques was working on the classic rape defense: she asked for it. He plodded on: "I don't think anybody can deny that there are flirtatious women. I don't think that anybody can deny that there are aggressive women, that there are devious women, that there are women who, when they like a guy, they will set out to get him in a devious way perhaps, perhaps in an aggressive way."

Now that he had attempted to set up Betty, her mother, and society as the criminals, Querques worked to portray his client and the rest of the gang as the victims.

"Were they abnormal or were they attracted to girls? Attracted to girls like ninety-nine out of 100 boys. Did they have knowledge of sex at sixteen, seventeen, eighteen? I hope so. There were times when—they don't do it anymore because now it's no secret—boys used to carry condoms in their wallet hoping one day they would get lucky and they would have the condom. Today you don't have to carry it around in your wallet, you don't have to hide it from your mother and father. Mothers and fathers and school teachers and boards of education are giving them to you for nothing, because they know what you are doing. They are just telling you to be careful about it. Did I make that one up? Or is that the gospel truth?"

At this point Querques outdid himself as he implored the jury to understand the events of March 1, 1989, in Kevin Scherzer's basement. "Boys, therefore," he preached, "have the same emotional and biological needs as did Betty Harris, and if there is any expression in the world that's the truth—maybe I coined girls will be girls—but everybody says, particularly if they have boys as children—you know what I am going to say now, don't you? Boys will be boys. Pranksters. Fool-arounds. Do crazy things. Experiment with life, and disregard their parents. Boys will be boys."

Were his defense arguments not so pitiful and condescending, Michael Querques would have seemed almost comical. A retarded Lolita took advantage of his innocent, curious client. But he still was not finished.

"What they had in common was they were friends. They were friends and friends take license. Friends are the ones you come to and say, Listen, I am in a spot, can you lend me five dollars? You know he is going to the race track and waste it, but you give it to him anyhow because he is your friend.

"People act differently among friends. You know if you went to a cocktail party, you don't know anybody there, you are acting one way; you go to a cocktail party where you know everybody twenty years, you are going to act different. You have to put that on the scale here."

Now Querques was ready to make his best move against society.

"There is another thing about this that they all had in common, that they shared with one another," and as he was picking up his stride against American culture, he added this strange remark: "I could lose my head. I hope I don't, I really hope I don't."

Kevin Scherzer was born in 1971, Querques told the jury. "If I use those two words, sexual revolution, did I make them up? I don't think so. I think any kid born in 1971, not in 1929 like me, but '71, if he goes into a candy store to get his father a newspaper, he sees anywhere between six and twenty girlie magazines, and if he has a couple of bucks, he buys one, he brings it home, and he looks at it at night, he looks at it in the bathroom, on the sneak. It's normal, natural behavior."

He addressed the jury as his peers. "When you were a kid, the only sex movies that you could see were, they had ones that were smuggled in from France, or you could write to a girlie magazine, make believe that you were an adult, and get it. You could go in 1971 to an x-rated movie, a pornographic movie, make believe you were eighteen, and get in?" It was another question and he had the answer. "You certainly could.

"This country—forget about Betty Harris—this whole country is obsessed with sex. You can't even turn on family television without seeing some guy in bed with some woman who is not his wife. You bring them up that way and then call them criminals? Huh?" Querques repeated his fantastic conclusion. "Bring them up that way and then call them criminals. Bring them up that way and tell them at eighteen, seventeen, sixteen, they should have the same judgment, the same expertise, the same knowledge, the discipline and the same courage that you do, to avoid it." And then a lascivious suggestion: "If you do ... If you do."

Querques turned again to his client. "The bottom line here is, in plain simple language—stand up again," he tells Kevin Scherzer. "He was a kid. Judgment. Judgment is one thing. Criminality. Doing something that's ..." Querques hesitates. "I was ..." he starts to say, and then, apparently losing his train of thought, "Forget it."

Quickly he was back on the prowl, reliving his own boys-will-be-boys days for the benefit of the shocked jury. "You think people are going to forget about the girls they knew in high school who were loose and the boys who took? Are men going to forget, Hey, I got a girl who is loose, do you want to join me? Go ahead, forget about it if you want, and then, when you go to bed at night, ask your conscience, Am I being fair to this kid?"

Next came another soliloquy about the availability of condoms in 1989 high schools. "I am not going to argue whether that's right or wrong. It doesn't matter for this case. The fact is that's the way these kids were raised, not by their parents, but by this new world we live in.

"You might want to turn back to the horse and buggy days, I know there have been occasions when I said I sure would like a horse and buggy. I don't need a Ferrari that goes 150 miles an hour, but they make them. I couldn't watch pornographic stuff on TV, cable TV, like these kids do."

Not quite finished, Querques turned back to Betty's mother and hardened his offensive against her. "If you know that the young lady is aggressive, if you know that the young lady in these simple terms has been fooling around for a couple of years, if you give birth control pills, you know sex takes two, you know the other half of the sex act when you have a female on one other half is always a male, consequently honor would dictate, decency would dictate, respect would dictate that if you were looking after Betty Harris you ought to do something to look after the young people she comes in contact with before you label them heinous criminals.

"But she wasn't kept home. She was normal as far as she was concerned, and the parents let her be as normal as she wanted to be, and if somebody else thought she was normal, too, and they did something with her, they are not criminals. They are not heinous, venomous criminals. It is a two-way street here. Everybody, but everybody needs protection."

Trying to impress on jurors that the basement incident was the fault of both Betty and her parents, Querques came up with a grotesque analogy, strangely enough, using a baseball bat to illustrate his story. "If I had a son who went around with a baseball bat breaking people's kneecaps, it is not enough that I take away the baseball bat, because he will go get another one. I better put a sign on him, I better warn his friends, I better warn schoolteachers, this kid has a capacity to break your kneecap with a bat. He just likes to do it."

Perhaps realizing he had gone too far, Querques admitted, "Now that's an absurd, absurd illustration, isn't it?" But he stuck with it. "It is not absurd when you bring it down to this thing that nobody likes to talk about and nobody wants to admit, and that is, young people have sex. They hide that. They hide that."

For more than two hours Michael Querques labored away at the jury. He was ready to sit down. "I don't have style," he conceded to the courtroom. "I do this to you, I do all these nutty things, but you have my message. Just be bright, be intelligent, love equality, and worship fairness in everybody."

"Thank you, Mr. Querques," deadpanned Judge Cohen, and the crowd supporting Betty Harris gasped.

■

In front of the courthouse, protesters marched with signs reading RAPE IS VIOLENCE NOT SEX. Ruth Jones, a lawyer for the National Organization for Women Legal Defense and Education Fund, told a reporter for the *New Jersey Law Journal*, "I can't imagine women on the jury would not be offended by this nonsense. This idea that men or women have sexual urges they are not responsible for controlling is totally absurd. If a woman has big breasts, she is basically a slut. That seems to be his theory."

As for the jury, several told the *New Jersey Law Journal*, after the verdict was announced, that they ignored Querques's entire off-the-wall opening argument during their deliberations.

7.

The
Trial
Observers

T he last weekend of spring after the verdict, a handful of middle-aged buddies is playing on the Glen Ridge High School baseball field. They are using a softball, practicing batting. They call back and forth to each other, encouraging hits, boasting, seeking to prolong their athletic youth. They know the famous local rape case in detail.

"What they did was wrong," Bob offers, "but I think they got too much." He's wearing shorts and no shirt and responds to questions easily in a mild, quiet voice.

His friend Jimmy comes up with another theory. "It was a white thing. The press got ahold of it and made an issue out of it." Jimmy is dressed in his weekend softball best: a skintight Mets T-shirt, a Mets cap, regulation baseball knickers complete with stirrups over his socks, and tennis shoes. "At that age, kids always rationalize things," Jimmy says. His body is still trim, but his blond hair is thinning. "You've heard of the herd mentality." And then he quickly adds, "Of course, what they did was wrong."

"And they let it drag on too long." Bob doesn't approve of the speed of the judicial process. "If they had settled it long ago, they'd be out by now."

Jimmy is still concerned about the affect race and the venue of the crime played in the case. "When you have a white affluent town, these things get blown out of proportion," he says. "If this happened in downtown Newark, the kids would've got out, no problem."

Their practice is on hold while the chatter heats up.

"That doesn't excuse it," Rick interjects vehemently.

"Of course it doesn't," Jimmy agrees.

A few more balls are hit.

"They should've gotten life," says Rick. He's gruff. His hair is gray, and his bare belly is pushing out of his too-tight shorts. "That girl is somebody's daughter. I have a twenty-four-year-old daughter, and if somebody did that to my daughter, I'd have 'em thrown in jail and have 'em fucking castrated."

They hit some more.

Jimmy's been thinking. "I think they got screwed."

"Oh, man," says Rick.

"They should get the one kid who orchestrated it," says Jimmy. "He deserved it. But the rest of them, it was the herd mentality."

"Jim," Rick says, turning to his friend. "What if it was your daughter?" Their debate continues, fueled by details about Betty Harris's personal history, details revealed because the intent of the New Jersey rape shield law was foiled.

"These kids' lives are ruined," says Jimmy—about the rapists. "I'm talking about the kids that suffered. The ones that said, 'Jeez, I didn't know what she was all about.'"

"It all comes out," he continues, ignoring the difference between consensual sex and rape, "It all comes out that she likes to fuck."

Rick is collecting the bats and gloves. Their play is over. "It's one thing to do that," he says, "and another to have a broomstick shoved up you."

"I'm a Protestant," is Jimmy's response. "I grew up in a good family. And when you grow up in a good family, you feel sorry for them. It's not like they grew up on the wrong side of the tracks."

■

In 1982, *Ms.* magazine published its first article on acquaintance rape. The article dealt with research conducted on the phenomenon at Kent State University by clinical psychologist Mary Koss beginning in 1978. With what was then popularly called date rape brought by *Ms.* to a wide national audience, the magazine and Dr. Koss received funding from the Center for Antisocial and Violent Behavior of the National Institute of Mental Health to conduct a scientific study of acquaintance rape. Called the *Ms.* Project on Campus Assault, the study's conclusions blasted devastating holes in Michael Querques's simplistic and uninformed defense arguments. The Glen Ridge rape was no fluke; it followed a pattern Dr. Koss and her fellow researchers found among misguided student athletes throughout the United States.

The *Ms.* study was compiled in the book *I Never Called It Rape.* Author Robin Warshaw's description of a typical gang acquaintance rape (written a year before the attack on Betty Harris) reads like an analysis of the Glen Ridge case. "Of course, participants in gang acquaintance rape rarely think of it as rape," writes Warshaw. "The woman is a 'nymphomaniac,' they will tell others later, who willingly engaged in what was nothing more than a spirited group sex adventure."

Warshaw continues with more disturbing parallels: "More often than not in gang acquaintance rapes, the group has carefully selected its victim. Sometimes she is chosen for her vulnerability or because she was sexual with a group member. On college campuses, she may be a newly arrived freshman student who may have few friends. The victim may be unpopular, unattractive, or simply naive and therefore easily flattered by the attention suddenly lavished on her before the assault begins."

Case studies cited in *I Never Called It Rape* include several instances of athletic team members acting together in acquaintance rape. Typical is one episode dating from 1986 at the University of California at Berkeley, where, after a football game, four freshman players engaged in sex with a dormmate. She called it rape; they called it consensual. The district attorney did not file charges; the university demanded apologies from the players and forced them to undergo counseling and perform community service.

A disconcertingly similar case was reported in a summer 1993 edition of the *San Francisco Chronicle*. Correspondent Dan Reed discovered that University of California at Berkeley police were in the midst of investigating reports that several football players raped, robbed, and battered a woman in Dormitory No. 2 on the Clark Kerr campus. Reed quoted police lieutenant Bill Foley as saying, "We have a very strong case. She has given us a very complete statement that we believe is very accurate."

"Like fraternities," concludes Robin Warshaw, "athletic teams are breeding grounds for rape, particularly gang acquaintance rape. They are organizations which pride themselves on the physical aggressiveness of their members, and which demand group loyalty and reinforce it through promoting the superiority of their members over outsiders." She recommends that schools add required courses in the dynamics of acquaintance rape—especially for star athletes.

The *Ms.* study and Warshaw's follow-up book are often cited for their terrifying statistics about rape. Offered as "facts" and summarized on the back cover of *I Never Called It Rape* are these numbers: 25 percent of women in college have been victims of rape or attempted rape. Eighty-four percent of these victims were acquainted with their assailants. Only 5 percent reported their rapes to the police. Only 27 percent of women raped identified themselves as rape victims. One in every twelve men admits to committing acts that meet legal definitions of rape.

These are sobering statistics. They are used by a variety of writers, politicians, and feminist activists to draw attention to what many are concluding is an epidemic of rape in America. Nonsense, says University of California professor Neil Gilbert. "I was walking to class one day and I picked up the *Daily Californian*," he tells me, describing how he became involved in trying to debunk the *Ms.* study. "There was a cover story saying 25 percent of the women on campus are victims of rape. So I walked into my class, a class of social policy graduate students, and I said, 'Doesn't this strike you as a harsh figure?' I thought we'd get a discussion on advocacy research. Instead I got a very chilling response of, 'Everyone knows that's the figure. It's at least that. Where have you been?' I said, 'One out of four?

That's really serious. We ought to have police all over campus.' We had a big argument in class, and I wanted to see where the numbers really came from."

Gilbert is not a rape specialist. As a professor of social welfare and social services at the School of Social Welfare of the University of California at Berkeley, he calls his academic publications "wonderful cures for insomnia." But he attacks the *Ms.* study vigorously, calling the research flawed. He is particularly offended by the conclusion that 73 percent of the women identified by the study as rape victims did not consider themselves victims until they were informed by the researchers that what occurred to them should be defined as rape. He dismisses as much too vague the survey questions "Have you had a man attempt sexual intercourse when you didn't want to by giving you alcohol or drugs?" and "Have you had sexual intercourse when you didn't want to because a man gave you alcohol or drugs?"

For his criticism of the *Ms.* study methodology and results, Professor Gilbert told me he was pilloried. "They had a vigil here," he says of his critics, "and a march, and they wrote a letter to the chancellor. Then I thought, there must be fire, there's all this smoke." Gilbert is convinced that the *Ms.* study is an example of advocacy research gone bad. "I think there was a concerted effort to raise consciousness," he says, an effort that included exaggeration. But he sees another motive lurking behind the *Ms.* report. "I think there is an ideology out there that says all men are pretty nasty beasts and therefore the research should show it. You can give me an answer to a question," Gilbert offers. "I'll formulate the question, and I'll do the survey, and I'll get you that answer, and that's essentially what it is."

As an example of a deceptive question he suggests, Have you ever had sex when you did not want to? "You ask that of a thousand people, you get a thousand yeses, and now you've found out everyone is getting raped and assaulted and victimized." Gilbert says the numbers he has studied tell him that there is no rape crisis in America. He suggests that over time the inflated figures will work against rape victims. "I think that if the notion that it's happening to everybody, that all women are raped and all men are rapists, becomes more widely spread about, the view of a jury could be, Why should we send this poor sucker to jail? Why should we send anybody to jail? It can't be such a big deal, it's happening to all the women."

Gilbert cites U.S. Justice Department figures from the Bureau of Justice Statistics, which uses surveys conducted by the Census Bureau. A sample of 62,000 households is studied every six months, and he likes the phrasing of their questions because the specificity of the inquiries leaves much less room for interpretation than do the more open-ended *Ms.* study questions. Gilbert's analysis of the Bureau of Justice Statistics figures shows rape and attempted rape declining by about 30 percent from the late seventies to the late eighties. He reads the bureau's findings as showing that, as the eighties ended, 1.2 women in 1,000 over the age of twelve were victims of rape. "No trivial number," he writes in a paper attacking the *Ms.* survey. He translates the number to a forecast that 5 to 7 percent of American women, or one out of fourteen, will be raped or be the victim of a rape attempt. "Assuming that the Bureau of Justice Statistics underestimated the problem by 50 percent," writes Gilbert, "that is, that it missed one out of every two cases of rape or attempted rape in the sample, the lifetime prevalence rate would rise to approximately 10 to 14 percent. Although an enormous level of sexual assault, at that rate the Bureau of Justice Statistics estimates would still be dwarfed by the findings [of the *Ms.* study], which suggest that one in two women will be victimized an average of twice in their life."

When Emilie Buchwald set out to collect essays for *Transforming a Rape Culture,* the advocacy anthology against rape she edited, she too was concerned about presenting credible figures. Like Gilbert, she went to the files of the Bureau of Justice Statistics and translated the 1991 figure of 171,420 reported rapes in America into "469 rapes each day of the year, or 19 each hour, or 1 rape every 3.5 minutes." The source and the numbers are the same as those used by Professor Gilbert, but Buchwald concludes from them that there is a crisis. "We will continue to live in a rape culture," she writes, "until our society understands and chooses to eradicate the sources of sexual violence in this culture."

Buchwald also sought help from the FBI's Uniform Crime Report, compiled from over 16,000 law enforcement agencies whose jurisdictions cover 96 percent of America. Despite the fact that rape is underreported to police, the FBI report recorded 106,593 rapes in 1991. "The definition of rape that these two surveys have is probably the most basic one that everyone can agree on," Buchwald told me as we discussed the figures and the crime. "It's forced penetration. It is exactly what anyone would imagine rape to be. When we talk about the continuum from remarks to touching to fondling, all the way up to rape—then we're talking about a rape culture." Buchwald is on a crusade with her book. "People can change," she told me. "A culture can change. If you look at sex as a source of pleasure—which I do—it's easy to see that rape, which is forced sex, has nothing to do with pleasure. Unless you confuse pleasure with domination, with inflicting pain and fear."

No matter whose figures are used, from the apparent hyperbole of the *Ms.* report to the conservative FBI numbers, rape is a crime plaguing Americans. The definition of just what constitutes rape is broadening and continues to be debated, as does the question of consent, and the Glen Ridge rape case is now an integral element of this escalating national debate.

■

"I don't think our society even views rape as a crime because there's no real punishment associated with it." Carol Vasile is anxious to talk about what the Glen Ridge case represents to women in America. Armed with the conclusions of the *Ms.* study and the exceptions allowed to the New Jersey rape shield law for the Glen Ridge defendants, the Essex County chapter of the National Organization for Women decided to send members Vasile and Christine McGoey to the trial of the Glen Ridge rapists as observers. Their assignment was to attend every single court session in order to keep track of anything news accounts of the case might miss.

Vasile and I meet at the Verona Diner, just a few miles up Bloomfield Avenue from Glen Ridge. Her coffee and English muffin get cold as she talks about the case, barely taking a breath. For six months, studying the Glen Ridge crime and speaking out against the rapists occupied most of Carol Vasile's days and nights, and her fervor for educating America about what she considers a rape epidemic is contagious.

"I'll have to tell you, I was absolutely shocked," she says about her experiences in the courtroom. "When I say 'shocked' it can't convey the emotions I felt sitting in that courtroom day in and day out. There are rape shield statutes on the books, but as you can see in the state of New Jersey, there's an exception you can drive a Mack truck through, it's so large. And it's all at the discretion of the judge."

For Vasile, the message from the defense at the trial and from the judge's light sentence was that the rapists were more important to Glen Ridge society than the victim. "It's not only that this was a woman who was raped; this was a mentally defective woman. It's almost like she's a throwaway. What difference does this make for her future?—this is what I think that mentality says." She continues to characterize how she perceives the thinking of those who supported the rapists. "What is she really going to do with her life anyway? I mean, after all, these are the promising young leaders of tomorrow."

From the beginning of the trial, Vasile and her colleagues felt the need to educate a sexist public that failed to understand what constitutes rape. "We were combating all these myths about rape. We had to hear that she was big breasted, she's a Lolita, she asked for it, she wanted it, it was her idea, she did it before, every myth that you could possibly imagine." In response, Essex County NOW printed a fact sheet and passed it out at the trial. It lists common misconceptions about rape and compares them with facts as compiled by NOW, but not documented:

MYTH: Only "bad" girls get raped. Fact: The FBI estimates that one out of every three American women will be raped.
MYTH: Rapes are committed by strangers in surprise attacks.

Fact: 80 percent of rapes are committed by someone the victim knows.

MYTH: Women provoke rape by their appearance or behavior —women who get raped deserve it. Fact: No one deserves to be raped. The impulse to rape comes from the rapist. Eighty-two percent of rapes are planned in advance. Rapists choose their victims based on availability and vulnerability, not attractiveness.

MYTH: Rapists are psychos—sick, "abnormal" men. Fact: "Regular guys" rape. In one study, 50 percent of college men reported that they would rape if assured they would not be caught or punished. In another, one in twelve college men surveyed admitted committing or attempting rape.

MYTH: Women falsely report rape. Fact: Exactly the opposite is true. Most victims NEVER report the crime of rape to anyone. Recent studies show that only 3 percent to 5 percent of all rapes are reported to the police. Conviction rates for rape are 1 percent to 4 percent. That means 99 percent to 96 percent of all rapists are walking free.

MYTH: Once a man is sexually aroused, he can't stop himself from forcing sex on a woman. Fact: Men, like women, don't physically need to have sex once they are aroused. Human beings are capable of controlling their actions and must be held responsible for them.

MYTH: If a woman doesn't physically resist, she hasn't been raped. Fact: Regardless of whether or not a woman physically resists, she has been raped if she has been sexually penetrated against her will. Police and rape crisis centers advise women to use whatever measures are necessary to survive rape, including going along with the rapist's demands.

MYTH: Women report rapes immediately. Fact: Most women do not report rape immediately after it happens. In fact, 42 percent of all rape victims never report rape to anyone. Those victims who do disclose wait until they discuss the attack with a "safe" person, a close friend, relative, etc.

MYTH: If no weapon is used, a woman hasn't been raped. Fact: Anytime a woman has sex against her will it's rape—

whether the rapist uses a gun, knife, drugs, alcohol, threatening words, physical isolation, his own body, tricks, or other forms of coercion.

MYTH: Non-virgins can't be raped. Fact: Anyone, including a sexually active woman, can be raped. Having sex on one occasion doesn't mean that a woman consents to sex with everyone on all occasions. Even if a woman willingly had sex with a particular man before, he has no right to engage her in sex against her will at a later time.

MYTH: A man who spends money on a date is entitled to have sex with her. Fact: Nobody owes sex to anyone in return for dinner or a movie, etc.

MYTH: A woman who agrees to kiss, "pet," or "neck" with a man also agrees to have intercourse with him. Fact: Everyone has a right to say yes or no to sexual activity of any kind. Engaging in one form of activity doesn't mean a person agrees to all forms of activity. No means no.

As she distributed the "Reality of Rape" flyers, Carol Vasile was shocked again by the need to dispense such information, by the ignorant audience she was facing. "We have a hell of a job to do," she says with some resignation creeping into to her energetic voice as we talk in the diner. "This was an issue twenty years ago. I think what a lot of people think is, 'Okay, we did our job. Now let's move on to the next issue.' It's almost like abortion. Around the same time, Roe versus Wade came through the Supreme Court. We had a ruling. These issues are resurfacing all over, as though we did almost nothing."

As Vasile and Christine McGoey sat through the proceedings, marched with other picketers in front of the courthouse, and distributed their leaflets, the other side responded. During court recesses, in the crowded hallways of the Essex County Courthouse, Vasile felt fear and intimidation as she encountered the defendants and their families, whose body language made their irritation with the NOW observers clear. The defense lawyers articulated their disgust. *New York Daily News* columnist Amy Pagnozzi reported that the defense commonly called Vasile and McGoey "the twin cocksuckers" and "the dyke brigade."

Carol Vasile takes another sip of her cold coffee. She is wearing a light sleeveless blouse to keep cool in the New Jersey summer. A silver chain hangs loosely from her neck, a silver heart dangling from the chain. Her intense, wide eyes are highlighted with a thin line of eyeliner. Sexism, she tells me, explains how and why so many people continue to rationalize the Glen Ridge rape.

"If you look at who was convicted of what—who was not convicted? Bryant Grober of most of the other crimes. He was not convicted of fellatio. Why was that? Now think about this." She does not wait for an answer because this is an argument she's intent on promoting. "That was the only thing that occurred in that basement that was even approaching, I think, what people consider within the normal bounds of normal sex. And he was not convicted. I think that is very fascinating, that the only acts that people were convicted of were penetrating the victim with a baseball bat, the broomstick, and these kinds of really horrible"—she searches for strong enough words—"you know, just the thoughts that you can conjure up in your mind when you hear a baseball bat and a broomstick and thirteen guys in a basement." Vasile's speech slows and her voice cracks. "That's horrible. And the victim's mentally defective."

But Vasile refuses to characterize the Glen Ridge rape as worse than others. "I don't see rape in degrees. I can't see it that way. To me, as a woman, when you're raped, what difference does it make? What difference does it make if it's one or a hundred?" She answers the question. "The only difference that I see it makes is when you're in the courtroom and you're beat within an inch of your life and you're black and blue, bruises all over, you're mentally defective, and someone violated you with a bat and a broomstick. Then that makes a difference because now the jury can say, 'Okay, it was rape.' But if it's an old lover, if it's your husband, if it's a brother, a father, one person, and you don't have a lot of bruises—is that any better?" Again, she answers. "I don't see that. I see you're still serving a life sentence for that rape."

Yet supporters of the rapists know Betty was victimized with the bat and broom, and still they see no crime. "It's the blame the victim mentality," says Vasile, and again she describes how she assumes the thought process works for those supporters. "It was her idea, she wanted it, she was doing it. And if we send our fine young sons away to prison, what will that do to the rest of their life? The hell with the rest of her life."

I ask Vasile to try to explain how someone could come to the conclusion that Betty would actually want a baseball bat and a broomstick inserted into her. "One of the things that I think is that this defense was a complete fantasy. I saw a completely male perspective. The way this defense was put on was particularly offensive. When this victim is on the stand and you're looking at her, she's as tall as an average woman would be, and then she opens her mouth, and you hear this very, very sweet, light voice—so childlike if you closed your eyes you'd imagine a very small five-, six-, seven-year-old sitting in that witness chair. The impact of just her sitting there and speaking moved so many people and, I'm sure, the jury."

She calls the defense not just a fantasy, but pornographic. "That anybody in 1993 would stand up in a courtroom and argue this kind of defense is beyond troubling. It's absolutely frightening. What would have been more frightening is if the jury bought it." Pornography, says Vasile, is where the defense would have to look to develop their claim that Betty Harris sought the attack perpetrated against her, and it was from pornography, she figures, that her assailants came up with their ideas for the assault. "Where are these ideas coming from? Where would a sixteen-, seventeen-, eighteen-year-old get an idea to penetrate a woman with a bat and a broomstick and set it up as if it's a theater for all your friends to be there? Is this a normal idea that you would think young people would have about sexuality? I don't think so. I think the idea of what women enjoy and what's okay comes out of pornography. It's not just *Penthouse* and *Playboy*, it's not just these kinds of things. It's regular everyday advertising, it's on the airwaves, it's on TV. It's how women are depicted, everywhere you turn around."

Vasile then makes a direct link between pornography and the defense tactics. "I can't imagine four women sitting at the defense table putting forward this defense, because we as women know that this is not true, that a woman would enjoy this. We as women know that this is not true. And you could tell," she says about her experience watching in the courtroom, "by exchanging glances, it was as though we were saying to each other, 'We all know this is the big lie, and we don't buy it.' Fortunately it got through to the jury as well."

In *The Beauty Myth*, Naomi Wolf offers up a multitude of examples of sexual violence entering the popular culture through movies, music, and books. Among the movies she cites are *Dressed to Kill, Tie Me Up! Tie Me Down!, Blue Velvet,* and *Body Double.* Her list of music titles that romanticize sexual attacks against women include the ode to the Boston Strangler heard on the Rolling Stones' hit "Midnight Rambler" and Trevor Rubin's "The Ripper." From modern writing she picks *Less than Zero,* a book by Bret Easton Ellis that Wolf sums up as "bored rich kids watch snuff films—and a preadolescent girl, bound on a bed, and raped repeatedly, is a background image throughout."

Wolf lists only mainstream materials. In the realm of hard-core pornography, films showing women masturbating with dildos are commonplace. The genre is known as single women movies, a famous title among aficionados is *Dildo Babes;* actress Ginger Lynn stars in several women-with-women blue movies featuring dildos.

Actress Linda Blair rates a footnote in the library of movies depicting women abusing women. Her classic is *Red Heat,* a soft porn epic in which Blair's character is raped with a stick in a women's prison by the leader of the pack of nasty inmates she had crossed. Blair screams as she is dragged from her bunk by the gang of women and thrown on her back, her naked legs forcibly spread apart. The ringleader approaches Blair, broom in hand, saying first sweetly, "Sophia makes you special," and then in rage, "Nobody fucks with Sophia." Rapes continue throughout the film.

In her book *Fraternity Gang Rape,* Peggy Reeves Sanday identifies the September 1984 issue of a magazine titled *Velvet* as an example of pornography that stimulates actual sexual abuse. The headline of the *Velvet* article targeted by Sanday reads, "Watch Our Cover Girl Take On Three Guys! Then Use Her to Create Your Own X-rated Action! Fucked Unconscious!" Sanday analyzes the article:

The photo fantasy showed several pages of three young guys, all college-aged, wearing oxford shirts and drinking beers and simultaneously having sex with the cover girl. At the end, "party girl" says to the reader: "Now, *Velvet* readers, you can stick it in me too! YOU Can Join This Action By Creating Your Own Hard-Core!" To facilitate "this action," a set of paper dolls is provided (the cover girl and two of the guys) and the reader is invited to join in the fun by playing with the paper dolls and making himself the third guy. It is suggested that a real woman might be substituted. Indeed, a letter is printed in the same issue that describes how the writer and his "buddies… had a great time playing the Fuck the Centerpiece game" from a previous issue with a "willing girl" who was there with them when they "played on one of the guy's" living room floor.

"This basic message that guys can have a great time together *if only* they can find a willing girl," writes Sanday, "is repeated over and over in the porno magazines and films that are consumed in quantity by some fraternity brothers."

Such examples are easy to find, and that is one reason why Carol Vasile does not consider Glen Ridge an isolated case. She sees pornography serving as instruction manuals for crime. "We're hearing about this Glen Ridge case, but how many other Glen Ridges were there? We're calling it a crime, but there's virtually no punishment, there's absolutely no punishment," she says about rape. "The majority of people who are committing this crime are walking free. This message had to get to these guys in Glen Ridge, just like it did to the Spur Posse and the Hardhedz Posse."

The message is seeping through society to lawmakers. A month after the Glen Ridge rapists were sentenced, the majority staff of the Senate Judiciary Committee released its report *The Response to Rape: Detours on the Road to Equal Justice*. The report details the results of a year-long investigation of state rape prosecutions and concludes that the justice system "fails by any standard to meet its goals—apprehending, convicting, and incarcerating violent criminals."

The statistics the report is based on were supplied by state and federal law enforcement authorities, and if it is accurate, an astounding 98 percent of rape victims not only do not achieve the satisfaction of knowing that their attacker is behind bars, they also fail to witness his arrest and trial (rape usually is a man-against-woman crime although man-against-man and even a few woman-against-man rapes do occur).

Of the remaining 2 percent, when an arrest is made and a suspect is brought to court, charges are dismissed or the suspect is acquitted in more than half the cases.

That leaves 1 percent of rape victims seeing their cases go to trial. Among that 1 percent, even when there is a conviction in court, almost a quarter of the convicted rapists avoid any prison time and another quarter serve less than a year in a local jail. That means that only half of convicted rapists end up locked up for more than a year.

In the report, Senator Joseph Biden, the chairman of the committee, uses the Glen Ridge case as evidence that the justice system is failing. "This," he writes about the light sentences and Judge Cohen's ruling that the rapists present no further threat to society, "is but one recent example of how our system discounts the severity of rape, how it 'normalizes' rape as the mistakes of errant youth or negligent men." It is, he asserts, a mistake and an injustice, "repeated day-in, day-out, in case after case, shaping women's perception that the system simply does not accept that violent acts against women are serious crimes."

■

Carol Vasile washes down a bite of English muffin with more murky coffee. "The jury had the courage to convict." Vasile is talking about Glen Ridge again. "The judge had absolutely no backbone. I can't even tell you the shock that I felt. It was like a shock wave went through the courtroom. I felt that everybody sitting there—you must have felt that as well," she says to me referring to that moment in the courthouse when the judge decided not to send the rapists to prison. "It was like being stunned, like somebody stunned the entire room. No one moved, no one said anything."

And she's correct; we were all digesting his complicated ruling at that moment, figuring out that the sentence meant the four rapists would walk out of the courtroom.

Once the shock wore off, Vasile came up with theories about why Judge Cohen made life so easy for the convicted rapists. "I think what he did was he was reaching to concoct a sentence that means nothing really." And why would the judge do such a thing? Vasile's answer is immediate: "Because he's seeing himself twenty-five years ago. He's looking at himself, and who does he see in front of him? He sees four clean-cut young men who have crisp white shirts on every day and nice suits. They come to court and their families are there. Isn't that a nice picture? And the victim? She's probably a slut anyway, right? Look, I mean they're the local high school football heroes. How can we send them to jail?"

■

New Jersey Superior Court Judge R. Benjamin Cohen was forty-eight years old during the Glen Ridge trial. He attracted attention because of the calm, removed attitude he projected in the face of the lawyers' histrionics and the overall high profile of the case. He presided over the court with quiet authority, not hesitating to become involved when he felt the defense and prosecuting lawyers needed guidance, but otherwise leaving them to do their work without interference,

During the trial, the *New Jersey Law Journal* polled lawyers not involved in the case—both prosecutors and defense lawyers—who were familiar with Cohen's work as a judge. The paper's conclusion: Cohen is described as "intelligent, articulate, fair, compassionate, and professional." The *Law Journal* published what it called a judicial survey in 1989, ranking Essex County judges on factors ranging from knowledge of the law to demeanor. Out of forty-five colleagues, Judge Cohen placed fourth.

A Newark native, raised in nearby Maplewood, Cohen studied at Dartmouth and then Rutgers Law School in Newark. He quickly worked his way up through the Essex County Prosecutor's Office, helped found the New Jersey Casino Control Commission, where he served as general counsel, and was promoted from there to his judgeship in 1981.

Judge Cohen enjoys an enviable trial record—few of the cases he has presided over ultimately have been overturned on appeal. Such a successful record adds to the mystery of Cohen's decision to allow the rapists to remain free on low bail during the years their appeals will drag on through the higher courts. As he passed the sentence, Judge Cohen said there were two factors involved in his decision to allow the four to stay out of prison. He was convinced they posed no further threat and, the judge stated, he would be "hard pressed to say there were no substantial" legal grounds to appeal the guilty verdicts.

Looking back on the six-month-long trial, Judge Cohen then announced that he was confident he'd made no mistakes and went on to add the line that was so devastating to Carol Vasile and other observers of the case, who'd expected and hoped the four rapists would go directly to prison once they were found guilty. "If I'm wrong," he said, "then the defendants will have spent a substantial amount of time incarcerated, perhaps unjustly." Judge Cohen lent further validity to Vasile's criticism when he characterized the Archers and the Scherzers as not "hardened or vicious" criminals and proclaimed them "not without redeeming value."

■

After another sip of coffee, Carol Vasile reflects again on Judge Cohen and his record. She is still amazed by what she heard in the courtroom, and she interprets it as representative of American society's built-in prejudices. "I mean, what did the judge say? He said, 'I can't imagine them doing this again'"—she mocks Cohen's presentation, using an emotionless monotone—"'and they come from intact families.' What does that mean?"

It's a question she answers directly. "If you're white and you're male, you have a free ride, you have an absolute free ride," she says with conviction. "Sitting in this courtroom day in and day out, every Monday we saw this judge sentence other people in other cases that were pending before him. I'm telling you, every single person before him that I was there to see was a young black man, except for one. And the one that wasn't, a young white man, who was his defense attorney? Querques. It was a death by auto case. He had killed his best friend. They were drinking." The story comes out fast and in detail. She remembers it vividly. "I forget what his sentence was, but it was less than a year."

Vasile takes the example story to her point. "Death by auto, you could argue that a lot of different ways. But every other young man, they were all adults, every single one got jail time. There were three men that I particularly took notice of. They were in their apartment, which happened to be within a thousand feet of a school. They had drugs. They had coke, I think. I don't know if it was coke or pot. Whatever. I don't know if they were going to distribute it or if they were using it. But they were arrested, and they were inside their apartment. I'm not an advocate for drugs, but what was striking to me is they got four years of imprisonment. For being inside your apartment with drugs? You get four years?" She cannot believe the inequity between this example and the resolution, by Judge Cohen, of the Glen Ridge case. "These guys brutally raped this woman, and they're walking free?" Her statements continue to come out like questions. As she retells the stories, Vasile still has trouble coming to terms with the sentences.

The low bail troubles her, too. "Even after they were convicted on first-degree offenses, the bail was never changed; there was no higher bail set. They're walking free. I think that the racism is astounding. If those were four young black men, they would have been hanged."

With resignation, Vasile adds one more element to her analysis of why crimes like the Glen Ridge rape occur. "There is no punishment. If you can do something, like if you can go up to this cash box in this restaurant and you can take all the money and walk out the door, would not a lot of people begin doing this? Everyone says, 'Well, that's stealing, that's a crime, you can't do it.' But if people are doing it regularly and regularly and regularly, and nobody says a word, you're never taught, it's never brought up, you never go to court, or if you go to court there's no punishment, is it a crime?" The answer is intense: "I believe so strongly that this society does not view rape as a crime. This is an epidemic. Where are the men? You said not every man has the attitudes of a rapist. Well okay. Where are the men, the men who don't have those attitudes? Where is the public outrage? I don't know why we are not marching down the street. I don't know why we are not demanding for this violence to stop. People say, 'Change is slow.' Well, you know what? I don't want to wait."

■

One of the many frustrating aspects of the Glen Ridge case is the lack of statistical information to back up or refute the oft-expressed belief that the Glen Ridge rapists would be serving long prison sentences if they were not rich white kids. The prosecuting lawyers told me they searched for proof of that theory, hoping to use it to move Judge Cohen to lock up the four once they were convicted, or at least increase their bail. But they and their staff were unsuccessful in their search. "Never for a first-degree sexual assault have I seen the convicted defendant get bail," said a puzzled and frustrated Robert Laurino.

"I think it is was almost reverse prejudice," Christopher Archer's lawyer, Thomas Ford, said, dismissing the charges of preferential treatment for the rapists based on their race and socioeconomic status. Ford called the sentences severe in light of his client's and the others' ages and criminal records. Without the spotlight of publicity, Ford said, the four would have received lesser sentences without prison time.

The closest evidence that there is at least some racial disparity in the manner rape cases are handled can be found in national figures compiled by the U.S. Justice Department Bureau of Justice Statistics. Data for 1988, the year before the Glen Ridge rape, from 300 counties were analyzed for the National Judicial Reporting

Program. They show that the incarceration rates for black and white convicted rapists are about equal: 86 percent of the whites convicted of felony rape in the seventy-five largest counties studied that year ended up behind bars, as opposed to 88 percent of the blacks.

There is at least one set of statistics in the report that tends to substantiate Carol Vasile's anecdotal conclusions. This result suggests that the whites convicted of rape probably serve easier and shorter sentences than blacks convicted of rape. While almost equal percentages of black and white rapists are locked up, the percentage of whites who serve their time in jail instead of prison is almost double that of blacks. This is a crucial difference, because although conditions vary from county to county and state to state, jail time is almost always preferable to prison time. Jail is defined as detention in a local facility. That often can mean an inferior physical plant and fewer positive educational and recreational opportunities for the inmate than at a state prison. But jail also almost always means fewer than twelve months behind bars. Jail means the inmate is less likely to be exposed to the tough criminal subculture that breeds in state prisons. Best of all, county jails often offer work-release programs that can translate into serving a sentence locked up only on weekends.

These statistics, of course, relate only to convicted rapists who are found guilty, sentenced, and imprisoned. What cannot be found are figures that determine if there is a racial disparity among the number of rapists found guilty and ultimately sent to either jail or prison. Also lacking in the statistical literature is a racial breakdown comparing suspects charged with rape with rapists eventually found guilty of the crime.

■

Carol Vasile pulls on her sweater—on the lapel is a button reading STOP THE WAR AGAINST WOMEN!—and before we say good-bye she pulls out a plain manila envelope, just one of the bags full of mail NOW received during the trial. Taped to the envelope is the NOW address, typed on a scrap of paper. The postmark is Glen Ridge. "It speaks to the fear and intimidation surrounding this case," says Vasile. "It was unpopular to speak out in Glen Ridge."

She dumps the contents of the envelope on the table, clipped-out photographs from the 1989 Glen Ridge High School yearbook—all pictures of the rapists frolicking through their senior year. And this note, complete with typographical errors:

You are right. This is how glen ridge looks up to its hero rapists. This is after knowing what they did to this girl. the kids in this school were intiminated by these bastards. Look at the pictures in the YearBook. The Principal of the school, girls who thought they were cute. Notice the caption under the Scherzers "We will always remember the experiences we have had." These guys got away with murder in this school. The administration is at fault. They treated girls like shit in the high school and everyone knew it.

—A former student

Mari Carmen Ferraez Fails to Save Her Boys

8

During their senior year at Glen Ridge High—the same year Kyle Scherzer raped Betty Harris—Scherzer dated his classmate Mari Carmen Ferraez. As the gossip and rumors and bragging spread around the intimate Glen Ridge High campus, Mari Carmen and the rapists realized that the incident in the basement at 34 Lorraine was taking on a longer life they originally expected.

The stickers that mysteriously appeared on hall walls at the high school with their slogans—MOLESTERS AMONG US and HA! HA! HA! YOU JOCKS'LL KNOW WHAT IT FEELS LIKE WHEN YOU GET RAPED IN JAIL—made it clear that the secret was out and that not all the school's 317 students were amused.

In September, Mari Carmen picked up her telephone. By this time it was clear her old boyfriend and his teammates were in serious trouble. Glen Ridge was being called the "Town of Shame" in tabloid headlines, and state prosecutors were working hard to get the rapists into state prison.

Twice Mari Carmen rang Betty's house. What Betty did not know was that Mari Carmen had hooked a tape recorder up to the line. Both of those conversations, as well as one that took place in November in a car and several others, were preserved on tape. The lawyers representing the Scherzer twins, Michael Querques and

Louis Esposito, hired a private detective to make the recordings in the fall of 1989. Mari Carmen pursued Betty, calling to talk about the events in the basement, taking Betty out for ice cream. Betty thought the attention meant the girls were basketball buddies. "She was a friend of mine," Betty would say later in court.

"Mari Carmen Ferraez was looked up to by Betty," prosecutor Glenn Goldberg told the jury as he outlined the State's case. "Mari Carmen Ferraez was one of the popular girls. Mari Carmen Ferraez was one of those girls that Betty would most like to emulate. She was a girl Betty trusted. She was an older girl. She was a co-basketball player. She was, to Betty Harris's way of thinking, a good friend."

It's just us girls talking, Mari Carmen lied to Betty as they chatted on the line. No one else will ever know about our conversation, she said, as she urged Betty to talk sex for the anonymous tape recorder while urging her to keep their talks a secret. New Jersey law makes such recordings legal as long as one party to a telephone conversation is aware that the call is being preserved on tape. Clearly the idea of the calls was to try to establish proof that Betty was a willing participant in the assault she suffered.

"If you listen to the tapes," Kyle Scherzer's lawyer, Louis Esposito, told reporters during a court recess once the trial was finally in progress, three years after the tapes were made, "they show that she understands sex, is conversant about sexual matters, and knew exactly what she was doing." But Esposito was upset. The prosecution was using the tapes against his client, using them to prove to the jury that Betty was unable to say no.

In one conversation, Mari Carmen tried to manipulate Betty into talking about the rape by telling Betty that she—Mari Carmen—was considering a trip to the Scherzers' basement herself for an encounter like the one Betty experienced.

"What a wonderful turn of events." Prosecutor Goldberg tried to explain to the jury how Betty would receive such questioning. "Imagine Betty now being befriended by this girl, this young woman. Suddenly there she is, a popular girl. Betty is being befriended and admired and respected, and as if that weren't enough, now Betty is going to be the teacher. She is going to teach

Mari Carmen Ferraez

this popular woman about sex in the basement at the Scherzers' home." Goldberg was preparing the jury for comments Betty made on the tape that could sound compromising.

"Was it fun?" Mari Carmen asked on the tape.

"Yeah, it was okay," was the answer from Betty.

Goldberg suggested to the jury that all the attention from Mari Carmen made Betty believe that the event in the basement "must have been some real adventure, something to be proud of, something to duplicate."

On another tape Mari Carmen asks, "Did you do the broomstick all by yourself? Like, if I wanted to could I do it? Like, did they let you do it yourself?" Again, she was trying to get a confession on tape that Betty initiated the use of the broomstick.

Instead, Betty answers her with a laugh and then says, "You want to do that to yourself?"

When she was finally on the witness stand, Betty was asked what she meant by her question to Mari Carmen. She meant, she testified, "why would anybody want to do that to themselves?"

The Ferraez tapes include this exchange: Mari asks, "Well, if you had to do it, if you had to do it all over again, would you go down again?"

Betty's response is, "I'd be scareder, I don't know."

Mari Carmen persists. "Like, if no one would ever find out about it, no one opened their mouths?"

"Yeah," says Betty.

Mari asks, "Would you do it again?"

"Yeah," says Betty, "if you went down with me."

Again, later in court, Betty was quizzed about her taped statement.

"Why did you want Mari to go down with you?" she was asked by prosecutor Robert Laurino.

"So she could see what it was like," explained Betty.

On the tapes, Betty is asked by Mari Carmen, "What else do you have to tell me about sex?"

And Betty answers, "Well, I don't know, just be careful."

Mari Carmen responds, "Be careful? Why do you say that?"

Betty's answer is so sweet and so sad. She tells Mari Carmen—the girl she considers a friend, the girl who is intent on manipulating her—"I don't want to see anything happen to you."

In another of the taped conversations, Mari Carmen tries to lead Betty with this: "Yeah, like have you ever gone up to a guy and then said, like, let's have sex, okay?"

But again she was foiled when Betty answered, "No, they usually come up to me, and they would usually say, let's do it, you know."

In still another failed attempt to get Betty to indict herself, Mari Carmen tells Betty that a man came up to her and said, "Let's have sex." Mari Carmen tells Betty her response was, "No, I don't want to," and she ran away. Mari Carmen laid her trap, asking Betty what she would do in an identical situation.

"I don't know," was Betty's answer.

On the tape is Mari Carmen's disappointed retort: "You don't know?"

"No," said Betty.

On the tape recorded in the car, Mari Carmen quizzes Betty about the frequency with which she engages in sexual relations.

"Whenever they're free, whenever they're around," Betty tells Mari Carmen, but exactly which partners she means by "they" is never made clear on the tape.

"Really?" Mari Carmen kept probing.

"Yeah," was Betty's response, "I feel like a whore but it doesn't bother me. I am so lucky. I mean, I've been doing this since I was little. I'm not pregnant. I'm not even diseased. I'm, I'm great."

Later on the tape, Mari Carmen reminded Betty exactly what was at stake as criminal proceedings against Mari Carmen's old boyfriend ground along.

"Now are you trying to get the boys in trouble, or you're not?" Mari Carmen asked.

"Well," answered Betty, "they got themselves in trouble."

"How?" asked Mari Carmen.

"Some kid actually told what happened," was Betty's simple reply.

For initiating the taped conversations, Mari Carmen Ferraez was indicted herself—for witness tampering. The charges were dropped months later, as part of a plea bargain, and for a while she remained on probation as she continued her studies in nursing. The tapes themselves proved of value to the prosecution's efforts to show that Betty lacked the understanding of both how to say no and the right to say no to unwanted sexual advances.

"The defendants played with Betty's body," said a disgusted prosecutor Goldberg, "but Mari Carmen Ferraez played with Betty's mind."

■

Betty was susceptible to being confused and manipulated not only by Mari Carmen Ferraez, who worked hard to become Betty's confidante, but "she could be easily led by anyone who chose to lead her," testified Jeanette DePalma. DePalma was one of Betty's teachers and a special education expert. "It would include people she wanted to like her," DePalma said about Betty's vulnerability to being influenced by others. "If someone treats her kindly, they automatically can become a friend. She has poor social judgment."

9.

Betty's Mother Testifies

K eep your voice up, so they can hear you," asks prosecutor Robert Laurino as Betty's mother finally takes the witness stand. Slowly her testimony traces Betty's childhood and school difficulties. Already a parade of prosecution witnesses had been used to establish Betty's vulnerability and mental deficiencies: Despite her studies in high school special education classes, her reading skills do not serve her well enough for understanding a basic restaurant menu; she cannot recall the names of four American presidents; she cannot follow directions for cutting a pie in half; she cannot follow movie plots or learn the starting time of a movie using the telephone. She believes that five states make up the United States, identifies the two major political parties in America as "public" and "primary," and, when tested by a psychiatrist hired by the prosecution, is unable to name the number that precedes 872.

"She's doing her own laundry now," says her mother as she describes Betty's tortured attempts to take some responsibility for herself. "She makes her bed. It's not up to my specifications, but it's made. We've tried teaching her how to use an oven, how to cook things."

But the family's success rate is minimal, and after Betty finally finishes her special studies at West Orange High School—never progressing past third-grade textbooks—there still is no possibility that she could live alone. "We do exciting things like minute rice, which had disastrous results. We've had tuna fish sandwiches, which sounds so simple, but she fixed it and was very excited about the fact that she had done it, and when you tasted it, you knew something wasn't right, and when I asked her what it was, she said, 'Well, I put that green stuff in.' And I asked what the green stuff was because I put in dried parsley. She put in oregano. It was green stuff, and that's the type of thing where you have to watch. But we're trying, we're hoping to have her part of a group home situation sometime, perhaps supervised apartment living."

She tells the court stories of frustration, one after another. "You can't just say, 'You go up and clean the sink,' because she'll put water in it or she won't use Comet or if she does, if you say, 'Now, be sure to use the Comet,' you have to be careful because you'll be scraping up the Comet. She puts it on too thick, everything gets covered. You have to literally do one step at a time and repeat it constantly."

Following directions and maintaining concentration were always problems for Betty. "You can't give more than two or three instructions," her mother tells the court. "If you say, 'Will you go upstairs and get my lipstick? It's in the right-hand drawer of my bureau. It's the third one down,' she would have no idea of what you were talking about. She'd get to the bureau, and then she would literally just keep opening drawers until she found it. The left and right are not always what she remembers, and she can't remember how many drawers you said."

Betty is unable to travel by herself, and she fails to understand the difference between cash and checks. "When she was in high school," her mother relates, "she wanted to buy her class ring, and we said, 'Well, you have to save your money,' and she had a summer job, and that was one thing she could save toward. It came time to pay for the ring, and I said, 'All right, we're going to the bank and take your money out and then I'll write you a check,' and so far she was agreeable. And we did that, took the money out, and I put it in my checking account and wrote her the check, and I think to this day she thinks I've stolen the money from her because she didn't have the cash to bring to school. I wasn't going to let her take the cash to school. But she could not understand that the check was the same thing as cash."

The questioning turned to the birth control pills prescribed for Betty. Her mother explained that she feared Betty might be raped in the sexually charged and anonymous atmosphere of Columbia High, and so decided to administer the contraceptives.

"Can you tell us how you explained to Betty what this medication was for?" Robert Laurino asked.

"I told her it was to regulate her period."

"Now around the time of March the first, 1989, when this alleged incident began—" it was time for Laurino to guide Betty's mother through her story of the rape—"did you notice any behavioral changes in Betty?"

"She was late," her mother said about Betty's arrival home the day of the attack. "In our house you have to be in at a certain time and the time is determined before you go out, and if there's a problem you have to call. She had not called, she was late, and I was angry. She was full of apologies, and I was still angry."

But there was no other suggestion of any problem until Betty went to bed. "She was extremely restless," remembered her mother, "and talked in her sleep, which she usually does not do. Her bedroom is right next to ours so I was aware of the fact that she was talking." The restlessness worried Betty's mother. "I went in and I couldn't understand what she was saying and tried to ask her, you know, 'What's wrong?'" But in response, all Betty initially offered were mumbles. "When I finally had her awake enough she said, 'Oh, nothing. Nothing.' And that's it. But the sleep pattern was what, looking back on it, should have given us some indication something had happened."

Carefully Laurino guided Betty's mother through her memory of that afternoon when Betty came home late, a recitation that eerily evokes the courtroom climax in Faulkner's *Sanctuary*. "Now, when Betty had come home that afternoon, did she bring anything home with her that you recall?"

"Yes, it was ..." and Betty's mother's voice trailed off, too quiet to be heard through the courtroom.

"What was that?" coaxed Laurino.

"It was a dirty red stick," repeated her mother.

Laurino took the tension off the moment with some routine work. "I'd like to have an item marked for identification."

The defense objected.

"Objection is overruled," decided Judge Cohen without hesitation. "It will be State's Exhibit 55."

The stick was then marked S-55, and Laurino asked Betty's mother to study it. "I'd like you to look at this item that has now been marked S-55 for identification purposes. Can you tell me if you can identify what that item is?"

Betty's mother continued to answer his questions quietly, with a controlled voice. "I believe that's the stick that was brought home," she said.

"Could you tell us," asked Laurino, "what you eventually did with that stick?"

"Stuck it on top of the refrigerator." At the time it was just another dirty stick to her.

"Do you recall why?"

"I was angry. I said, 'Why are you bringing the dirty stick home?' and to get it out of the way, I took it away from her and stuck it up there. It's higher than I am, and I didn't see it then, just got it out of the way."

"Could you tell us then what you eventually did with the stick?"

"Well, when we were made aware that there had been a problem, we were called down to the police station. This was one of the things that came out, that there had been some kind of a stick involved and all I could think of was the stick that I had taken away. I brought it down to the police station and said, 'This is the stick that she brought home.'"

Once Betty's mother was informed by school officials that some sort of sexual encounter occurred between Betty and a group of Glen Ridge boys, she made an unsuccessful attempt to ask Betty to tell her what happened.

"She does not like discussing things with us in general. She does not like discussing sexual things with her father present," Betty's mother explained. "So we get a sort of a, 'Nothing happened, it's okay. Don't worry.'" The chat was a failure.

The direct examination concluded, and the defense lawyer Thomas Ford, representing Christopher Archer, stood up to begin the cross-examination. Early in the trial, Ford became famous for his meandering questions and speeches that seemed to head toward no particular point, for his dandy appearance, and for the affectations he choreographed into his parades around the courtroom. "He strikes these mock-sartorial poses," wrote Amy Pagnozzi for the *New York Daily News*, "one of which—right hand on hip, left arm raised, wrist dangling—reporters dubbed his 'Full Teapot.'"

"I didn't mind that," Ford told me after the trial. "Clinton gets mocked, Bush got mocked. If you're in the public eye, people can put what they want in. That doesn't bother me. I know how effective I am or ineffective. So what people say doesn't bother me."

Ford worked Betty's mother hard, as he established that Betty was sexually active prior to the Glen Ridge rape. He led her through the decision to prescribe birth control pills for Betty and Betty's expulsion from a summer camp. "She was in a coed camp for the first time. It was an overnight camp, and I believe on the way to the dining hall she had, I don't remember specifically what was said, but it was inappropriate conversation with one of the boys."

Ford tried to lead her through the story that she raised her blouse and exposed herself while a student at Columbia High School. "Now, when Betty was in Columbia High School, were you ever made aware of by any of the faculty members the fact that during a class Betty had exposed her breasts?"

Betty's mother seemed surprised. "Exposed her breasts?" she asked Ford.

"Yes," he said.

"Not that I recall," she answered. "And I think that I would recall it."

Ford moved through Betty's friendships, her jobs, her walks around Glen Ridge, and then asked, "Can we have that red stick?" calling for the evidence. "The other day you were shown a stick that's marked S-55 for identification. Do you recall that?"

"Yes."

"Now, you stated, I believe, that you placed that on your refrigerator on March 1, 1989."

"Yes."

"Did you move it, at all, at any time prior to the time that you turned it over to the police?" Ford asked.

The response provoked a moment of lightness amid the tragedy. "You're making me tell secrets that I don't clean the top of my refrigerator. No."

"You don't clean the top of your refrigerator?" said Ford.

"Unfortunately, it's taller than me and I don't see it."

"So there may be lots of things up there?" asked Ford.

"Yes."

"So this just was one of many?" Where Ford was going was unclear.

"Yes."

"So there was no particular significance to your putting it up there?"

"I put it up there to get it out of the way," she explained.

"And that was the only reason?"

"That's all."

"And then you turned it over to the police at one point?" he asked.

"Yes."

Ford pressed on. "Was there anything particular about the shape or color of that stick that made that particular stick remain in your mind?"

"When?" she asked, confused.

"I mean the color or the shape," he explained.

"You mean when she brought it home?"

"Right."

"I just took the stick," she reiterated. "I was angry. She was late. I said, 'What did you bring that dirty stick home for?' and took it away and put it up there. That's all I did."

Finally it became clear what Ford was trying to uncover: that months after first reporting the rape, Betty changed her story regarding the stick and one of the thirteen boys in the basement,

Richie Corcoran—eventually telling her mother and prosecutors that Corcoran did not penetrate her with the stick. Delays in reporting and inconsistencies between initial and later reports are common among rape victims. These breakdowns are examples of rape trauma syndrome.

Alan Zegas, the lawyer for Bryant Grober, took over the cross-examination. Of the four defense lawyers, he was the least experienced; this was his first trial at the state court level. Zegas directed his questions to Betty's conduct at Columbia High. He read a report from one of Betty's special education teachers: "This year she made most inappropriate verbal sexual advances to members of one of the sports teams to get their attention. Her counselor and I have talked to her about this behavior. We will continue to have discussions with her about expressing her feelings in a more acceptable manner. Betty's gym teacher and I have also had discussions with her about smoking at school. Again, this has been, on Betty's part, to get attention. She's accepted cigarettes to be part of the gang."

Betty's mother told Zegas the report was unremarkable "because if it were something major, then it would have been something that we would have had parent conferences on and so forth. This is part of a review which we get periodically, and the teachers were handling it. So it shouldn't have been anything extraordinary. We knew that she had socially unacceptable behavior."

Zegas repeated the story about Betty lifting her shirt, told another that alleged she participated in a sex act in a school closet, and asked if the real reason Betty left Columbia was not that school officials worried she was in danger there but that "she was making inappropriate remarks and doing inappropriate things in school sexually that the school couldn't tolerate."

Betty's mother suggested the shirt-lifting incident was what occurred in the closet and could be explained by Betty's lack of understanding of appropriate behavior for her chronological age, not sexual expression. "She often wears a T-shirt and a sweater or a sweatshirt and a sweater. She was taking it off and the T-shirt came up. We had long discussions about how to take off your clothes. Because if you're warm and you start to lift up your blouse or sweater, whatever comes underneath comes up as well."

Zegas kept at her, insisting that Betty was abruptly removed from Columbia High not because, as her mother continued to testify, her parents and school officials worried that she was in jeopardy, but because her own displays of sexuality were disruptive. "The fact is that Betty was not a potential rape victim. Betty posed a danger to the welfare of some of the other students at the school because of her inappropriate conduct. Isn't that true?"

At that point the prosecution objected. "Once again," complained Glenn Goldberg, "Counsel is arguing with the witness. It's not an appropriate question. It's mere argument."

"I'll allow the question," ruled the judge. He turned to the witness. "Is that so?"

"We had never been told that, sir, no," Betty's mother answered. "The situation was that she was a potential rape victim."

"Although those words don't appear in any one page of the thousands of pages of reports that you turned over to us. Is that correct."

"That's correct."

Goldberg interrupted again: "Objection to repetition."

"You are going over this," the judge agreed with Goldberg's criticism.

■

After Betty propositioned classmates for sex, repeatedly engaged in inappropriate conversations with sexual themes, and was touched on her breasts in a classroom on at least one occasion, Columbia High counselor Carol Bolden tried to teach her that "her body was very, very private. She didn't understand that. In her mind, a friend is a friend. If a friend comes up and touches you, that's a nice thing." But Betty "loved attention and would speak in sexual terms to get attention" even though, testified Bolden before Betty's mother took the witness stand, she had "no understanding of those terms." Bolden tried to teach Betty. "She had a right to say no, and she certainly needed to learn the way to say no." But Bolden was unable to teach that simple necessity to Betty.

Betty was removed from Columbia at the request of the school, said counselor Bolden, not only because of her "inappropriate" socializing. She was not progressing academically past a second-grade reading level, and she was reclassified from "neurologically impaired" to "mildly retarded."

"She has the body of a woman and the mind of a first-grader," concluded Bolden. "She was asked to leave because she was a mentally retarded student whose needs were not being serviced in the building. She was extremely vulnerable in the building. We could not guarantee her safety." Betty's judgment was definitely a special concern. "I have a concern about any student who's unable to comfortably say no."

■

"Okay, Your Honor." Zegas changed his line of questioning, asking Betty's mother, "When was it that the incident that is the subject of this trial was brought to your attention by any authority?"

"I believe it was almost a week after it occurred, or at least several days after it occurred."

"Either on March 8 or March 9, 1989, you were advised that there might be some problem involving your daughter? Correct?"

"Yes, I believe it was...."

Zegas continued, "And you were given that advice by somebody in the school system, correct?"

"Yes."

"And who was that?"

"Mr. Clark, I think his name was, spoke to my husband," she answered.

"And I think you indicated in response to cross-examination by Mr. Ford that what you were told initially about what might have happened on March 1, 1989, was, in your words, 'very vague.'"

"Correct," she said.

"Were you told," Zegas asked, "by Mr. Clark that your daughter had complained that on March 1, 1989, somebody put a 'drumstick' in her 'butt'?"

"I believe that's what we heard," Betty's mother agreed. She told Zegas that she and her husband "spoke to Betty about it and asked what the story was, and she said, 'Oh, nothing happened. Nothing happened.' She denied the whole thing. When we pressed her, she said something about, 'There was a problem in the park,' or something like that, or '"Somebody put their hands in my pants."'

Later in March, Betty's mother testified, about two weeks after school authorities first suggested that there may have been a problem, the Glen Ridge Police finally sent a detective to the Harris home. During the intervening period, Betty went with her mother to her gynecologist, Dr. Robin Meglia.

"Now, what was your purpose in going to visit with Dr. Meglia?" Zegas asked.

"Well, if she had been violated in some way, we wanted to find out if she was all right."

"Did you have a discussion with Dr. Meglia before she examined your daughter?" asked Zegas.

"I think I told her there was a possibility of a rape situation."

"But that was never conveyed to you, was it?" Zegas demanded. "All that you were told was that Betty thought she might have—that somebody might have put a drumstick up her butt or somebody might have been touching her panties. Correct?"

"Right."

"When you went to Dr. Meglia's office," Zegas pressed on, "did you say, 'Dr. Meglia, the reason I am here today with my daughter is because there was a possible rape situation. I got a call, and I'm real concerned about it'?"

"I think I did. I think I did say that we are concerned, we're not sure and that this is what we want her examined for."

"If you thought there was a potential rape, wouldn't your first inclination be to call the police?"

"No," said Betty's mother.

Alan Zegas then took Betty's mother back to the doctor visit, and made use of the opening the court provided the defense to waive the total protection potentially afforded by the rape shield law.

"Do you recall," he asked, "saying to Dr. Meglia that Betty had an incident with fondling recently?"

"Could be."

"And that a boy put a finger in her vagina?"

"Could be."

"Did you tell Dr. Meglia, 'The reports we're hearing, Dr. Meglia, are that a drumstick was put into the rectum of Betty. We want you to examine to see if there is any evidence of that'?"

"I don't know if I specifically said a drumstick, but that she had been molested."

Zegas then showed Betty's mother the medical records of the visit and said, "What it does say is that a pelvic was performed and the results were within normal limits. Correct?"

"Yes."

At this point Zegas made an effort to convince the jury with medical records what Querques had attempted to prove with crude language and innuendo: that Betty was sexually active and sexually aggressive and that the activities in the Scherzers' basement were not rape, but mutual sex play and experimentation.

"At the top in the second line of the report," said Zegas, "it says that Betty is here to resume birth control pills. Correct?"

"Right."

"And beneath that it says, 'Had incident and fondling recently, boy put finger in vagina,' with a question mark. Is that correct?"

"That's correct."

Zegas wanted to know why there was no record of a rectal examination. Betty's mother said she assumed it was included in the overall procedure. Zegas asked her about her previous testimony during Ford's cross-examination. Why had she told him that she and her husband were "scared to death" and consequently ordered birth control pills for Betty?

"You weren't scared to death at that point"—Zegas tried to trap her—"because you didn't even know whether in fact anything had occurred at that time."

Betty's mother disagreed with his conclusion. About the initial reports that some type of sexual incident occurred, she said, "It makes you aware that she is extremely vulnerable, and that is why she was on the birth control pills. Whether anything happened or did not happen at that point, things could happen and that's why we went back to Dr. Meglia and resumed the use of birth control pills. I do not like medication. She had been on it for a year." This was not a revelation to the jury; Betty's gynecological records had been described by lawyers from both sides. Her mother explained that over a year before the assault with the bat and broom—because of concern that she was sexually vulnerable—the contraceptives were part of her routine. "When we found out there could be a possibility of anything," her mother said about the early reports of rape at the Scherzers', "whether it was this situation or anything else, we went to the doctor and said, 'We realize there's a vulnerability, we want something done.'"

Zegas demanded, "You still contend that when you sent Betty to Dr. Meglia on December 28, 1987, your reason for going to get birth control pills for your daughter was because she was a potential rape victim and not because she, of her own accord, was having sexual relations with other men?"

"I have never heard that before," was Betty's mother's firm response.

"She was vulnerable because she acted in ways that were inappropriate," Zegas insisted. "Isn't that correct?"

Betty's mother held her ground. "She was always vulnerable because people can manipulate her."

"I'm just asking"—Zegas tried to mitigate the conflict between them—"but she can also be very forward in a sexual way with people that she doesn't know well or with people that she doesn't know. Is that correct?"

"She has inappropriate conversations," her mother acknowledged. "It is not always sexual, sir."

Another long trial day concluded. "I want to excuse you, members of the jury," Judge Cohen announced. "We're going to break now for the day."

■

When he rose to make his final arguments, Michael Querques lashed out at Betty's mother again, blaming her for the crime, charging that she lied when she testified that Betty's active sex life was unknown to her. "The one word I get sick of hearing," he stated, "is she's 'vulnerable.' What did you do about her vulnerability?" He was addressing the jury, but speaking as if he were questioning Betty's mother. "You didn't warn anybody. You share part of the blame. Bottom line," concluded Kevin Scherzer's lawyer, "if it wasn't these boys, it would have been others."

Querques ranted for more than four hours as he reprised the arguments he used for his opening speech. "These four boys are your brothers," he told the jurors. "I'm not letting anything happen to them, not as long as I'm alive, not as long as I have an ounce of energy." Querques, identifying Betty as "the so-called victim," insisted, "This young lady was ready, willing, able, and anxious to go into that cellar, to get attention, to get affection. She bartered for it and she'd go back because she had fun. Those are her words. They are not mine."

Betty, he said, was "the best witness for these boys that I could ever imagine."

Betty
Takes
the
Stand

10

J ammed full with spectators for the first time since the trial started, Judge Cohen's courtroom was unusually still as Betty Harris sat down on the witness stand. There was no chitchat from the audience; even the news reporters were quiet, carefully watching the victim and the rest of the players.

Almost four years had passed between the assault in the Scherzers' basement and Betty's public appearance in the Essex County Courthouse. But before she finally was sworn to tell the truth, Judge Cohen tested her; he needed to determine whether or not she could differentiate between truth and untruth. The defense petitioned the judge to keep her off the stand because of retardation. "The question that has to be answered in the end," said Bryant Grober's lawyer, Alan Zegas, "is whether she understands the oath and the consequences of lying." Under New Jersey law, judges may disqualify witnesses as mentally incompetent if they cannot make themselves understood or if they do not understand that after swearing to tell the truth, they must tell the truth.

"Hi, I'm Judge Cohen," he greeted her at the competency hearing and asked her a series of questions. "If I say my robe is black, is that the truth?"

"Yes," said Betty.

And if he called it red, would that be the truth? he asked.

"No," she answered.

"If I say I'm standing up," said the sitting judge, "is that the truth?"

"No," said Betty, "You're sitting down."

Judge Cohen asked if it would be the truth to call Betty's sister Judy. Judy is not her sister's name.

"No," was the answer again, and Betty told the judge that it is "bad" to lie.

■

"We're going to ask you some more questions," Judge Cohen told Betty after he ruled she could testify. "Will you answer all of our questions for us?"

"Yes." Betty's answers throughout her testimony would be short and simple. She sat in the courtroom wearing a sweater and slacks, sometimes fooling with a bracelet, her hair cut short. She would not be called pretty: "plain and plump" was the description used by *New York Times* reporter Jane Fritsch that day. "Tall, stout with a baby face and a child's demeanor," suggested Fritsch's colleague at the *Times,* Robert Hanley. Across the courtroom sat the four defendants, their chiseled, hard faces accentuated by their conservative business suits and their rigid posture. It was the first known encounter between Betty and the four rapists since the crime. Throughout her testimony, the four of them stared at Betty without discernible expression. But it was a severe look, criticized by the prosecution as an attempt to intimidate Betty. Only periodically did she look across the courtroom in their direction.

"Let's bring the jury out," ordered the judge and, once they were seated, he greeted them. "Good afternoon, again, members of the jury. All jurors are here," he said for the record. "Prosecutor, you may call your next witness."

"Thank you very much," said Robert Laurino. "The State calls Betty Harris."

"Please swear in Betty Harris," ordered the judge, and Betty swore to tell the truth.

"Betty," Laurino addressed her directly. "Is it okay if I call you Betty?"

"Yes," was the answer.

"Okay, thank you," said Laurino. "Now, we're in a courtroom, and there's a lot of people here so I want you to keep your voice up so we can hear all the way back where I'm standing, okay?"

Again a simple, "Yes."

"First of all, Betty, can you tell me, when is your birthday?"

"May twenty-fourth," she answered.

"And what year were you born in?"

"1971."

"Can you tell me where you were born?"

"Newfoundland, Canada."

"Do you know where that is?" asked Laurino.

"That's in Canada."

"And do you know where Canada is?" he asked.

"No," she said.

Laurino continued with similar questions, eliciting basic answers to simple personal questions about family, school, and home. He asked about her swimming and softball, her nephews and her work with children at the local Head Start.

"What do you do with the little children?"

"Play with them," Betty explained. After just a few questions, it was evident to the most casual observer—and certainly to the jurors—that Betty's mental development was arrested.

"Okay," Laurino said. "Now, Betty, I want to talk to you about something that happened back in March, okay, March the first of 1989. Is that okay?"

"Yes."

"Okay, now Betty, I want you to think all the way back to that day, and did you go to school that day?"

"I think I had half a day."

"And when school was over, where did you go?"

"I went to the park."

"And do you know the name of the park?"

"Carteret."

"Okay, did you ever go to the park before?"

"A couple of times."

"And when you went to the park, did you go by yourself or did you go with other people?"

"I went by myself."

"And when you went to the park, did you bring anything with you to the park?"

"I brought my radio, I brought a basketball, and a stick I found in the park."

Spectators leaned forward. Laurino asked Betty to keep her voice loud enough to be heard throughout the tense courtroom.

"Okay," said Laurino. "I want you to take a look at something that we already have a number on, and the number here is 55, okay? Take a look at that, Betty, and do you know what that is?"

"That's the stick I found in the park."

"Okay," said the prosecutor. "Now Betty, when you found the stick in the park what were you doing with the stick?"

"I was throwing it."

"Okay, and when you threw the stick, what would you do after you threw the stick?"

With her brief response, the jurors were reminded of Betty's low IQ, of her third-grade, eight-year-old's mentality.

She said simply, "It would land."

"Okay, and then what did you do, pick it up again?"

"Yes."

"And throw it again?" Laurino asked.

"Yeah."

"Now Betty, when you got to the park, was there anybody else at the park when you got there?"

"Well, there was a couple of people."

"Okay." Laurino guided her: "Now, why did you go to the park, Betty, what were you going to do at the park?"

"Play basketball, mostly," she said.

"Okay, and when you said there were some other people there in the park, what were other people doing?"

"Well," Betty remembered, "some of them were playing basketball, and some of them were, like, throwing the ball around, like a baseball."

Betty identified the people at the park one by one. Richie Corcoran, Paul Archer, Christopher Archer.

"And what were these guys doing while you were in the park?" asked Laurino.

"Hanging out," she said.

"Keep your voice up now, okay?" encouraged Laurino as he moved to the crucial initial encounter between the boys and Betty.

"They came over and talked to me," Betty told him. "It was Peter..." She hesitated.

He helped. "Okay, what's Peter's last name?"

"Quigley" she said. "There was—there was—I can't remember."

"Think real hard," encouraged Laurino. "Put on a little thinking cap, okay? Think hard. Who came over and talked to you in the park? Was it more than one boy?"

"Yes." Her voice was softening again, and as the crowd in the courtroom strained to hear, Laurino asked her speak louder. She identified Bryant Grober as another of the boys in the park and said they greeted her, asking her how she was doing and what was up.

Lawyers for the defendants stopped the questioning and objected to what they considered Laurino's leading questions. Phrases like "think real hard," they complained to the judge, were inappropriate. But Judge Cohen allowed the prosecutor to continue because of Betty's mental limitations. "If the witness indicates that's all she can recall," ruled the judge, "that's one thing. But if she indicates, for example, as she has, that there was a group of boys and she only remembers one name, and then she's asked to think harder, and she comes up with another name, and asked again she's able to remember more names, I'm going to allow that, given the purported limitations of the victim."

Laurino asked Betty what the boys said to her, and her first answer was, "Nothing." Then she added, "Oh, wait, wait, wait, there's something else. I remember that they said if I ..." She stopped and started again. "Oh, they said ..." Either she was having a hard time remembering, or she was reluctant to say in the packed courtroom what occurred next. "Well, before we left, they said that …" Bryant Grober's lawyer, Alan Zegas, interrupted, complaining to the judge that no specific question was pending. But the judge overruled the objection, and Betty continued, finally ready with a complete statement explaining her departure from Carteret Field.

"They said," Betty testified with difficulty, "that if I go down to the basement, they said when I go down to the basement…" She tried again: "They said when I go down to the basement I'd go out with Paul Archer."

"Okay," Laurino told her. "Do you remember who said that to you?"

"Grober said that."

"And Betty, where did you go from there?" asked Laurino.

"I went to the Scherzers' house."

Again her voice was hushed. Kevin Scherzer's lawyer, Michael Querques, complained, "We really can't hear a word, Judge."

Judge Cohen turned to Betty and encouraged her. "I know it's hard to keep your voice up, but please speak loudly, okay?"

"Okay," said Betty, and at Laurino's request she identified the Scherzer house in a color photograph of the neighborhood.

"Now, when you walked to the Scherzers' house," he asked, "how did you walk, by yourself or did somebody walk with you?"

"I walked with Chris."

"Okay, and how was Chris walking with you?"

"It was like…" Betty thought back to the feelings she had as Chris led her to the basement. "It was kind of romantic," she concluded. Laurino asked for a further explanation. "It was romantic because he had his arm around me, and we walked down to the basement together."

"And did Chris say anything to you when he was walking with you?"

"No."

"Now, when you went downstairs into the basement, do you remember if anybody was there?"

"There was a lot of people there," Betty answered, and she identified members of the gang and described the appearance of the basement. "It had chairs, like lounge chairs, like, you know, sitting chairs. There was a refrigerator, and then there was this big, huge couch." As she arrived, chairs were being arranged in front of the couch. "It was set up like a movie," said Betty.

"Did you just stand there in the basement?" asked Laurino.

"No, I sat down on the couch."

"Okay. When you sat down on the couch, was there anybody else on the couch?"

"Not at first." Betty's answers continued to be brief, just a few words for each response. Most news reports of her testimony mentioned the childlike singsong of her voice as she recounted the attack. She often did not sit still. She sometimes frowned and at other times turned red as she pieced together her story. During private talks the judge engaged in with the lawyers, conferences that interrupted her testimony and left Betty alone on the stand, she seemed confused, at times casting a look at the defense attorneys and at times hiding her head in her arms.

Eventually Bryant Grober joined her on the couch, Betty testified. "They told me to do something."

"Okay," said Laurino, "let's start with that. What did they tell you to do?"

"Finger myself."

"Okay. And when they told you to finger yourself, what did you do then?"

"I did it."

"Okay. Now, what do you mean when you said you fingered yourself?"

"Well," Betty told him, "you put your hands in your vagina."

"Betty," he asked, "how were your clothes then when you had to finger yourself?"

"They were off."

"How did they come off?"

"I took them off."

"And were all your clothes off at that time?"

"Yes."

"And now, when you are fingering yourself, Betty, is anybody saying anything?"

"They're saying to put five fingers up your vagina." Laurino asked her if there was other talking from the basement audience, and she testified, "They said go further, further, further."

"Now Betty," Laurino asked, "then when you are all done doing that, could you tell us what happened next?"

"Well, then came Brian Grober," she said, misstating Bryant's name.

Laurino let the unimportant error stand uncorrected. "Okay," he said. "Tell us then about Bryant Grober, how did that happen?"

"Well," she said, characteristically direct, "he told me to suck his dick."

"And could you tell us what happened at that point?"

"I did suck his dick."

"And when you are doing this, is there any talking going on?"

"They were saying, 'Go further, further, further.'"

Laurino asked, "Can you tell us, where were Bryant's hands when this was going on?"

"On my head," she reported.

"And could you show me, Betty, could you use my head?" Laurino was trying to prove that Grober used force.

But Betty was blushing; finally—with a roll of her eyes to communicate her discomfort with the re-creation—she let out a frustrated breath and placed her hand on top of Laurino's head. Then she pushed down firmly.

"Betty," Laurino asked, "when that happened, was something inside your mouth?"

"His balls."

"And where exactly was your face at this point?"

"It was on his balls."

"And where was his penis?"

"In my mouth."

Laurino asked Betty about event after event, eliciting her terse recitation of her basement ordeal.

"Then came the broomstick," said Betty when Laurino asked what happened next. "It was fire-engine red," she remembered, and she identified Kyle as the boy who procured it. "He put Vaseline and a bag and a rubber band over it," she said, "and he gave it to his brother Kevin. He stuck it in me."

"Where did he put the broomstick?" Laurino wanted specifics.

"In my vagina," and again she said the chorus was chanting, "Go further, further, further."

"Was there any name-calling going on," Laurino wanted to know, "anybody calling you names?"

"They were calling me Pigorskia," she said. It was a variation on the pejorative nicknames the same group of classmates had taunted Betty with since kindergarten.

"Then came the bat," testified Betty. "Kyle gave it to Chris," she said, after he "put Vaseline on a plastic bag and a rubber band over it." She was shown a fungo bat identical to the one used against her and was asked which end of the bat was covered. Betty identified the handle end of the bat and said Chris "stuck it up my vagina."

"Now," Laurino said to Betty, "we've talked about the blow-job and we've talked about the broomstick and we've talked about the bat. Could you tell us what happens next?"

"Then comes the tiny little stick," said Betty.

"Which stick is this now Betty, where did the stick come from?"

"The park."

"And who had the stick?"

In October 1989, seven months after the rape, Betty drew these pictures of the assault during an interview with Dr. Ann Burgess, a psychiatric nurse and professor at the University of Pennsylvania. Dr. Burgess testified at the trial that the drawings show Betty suffered from rape trauma syndrome, a disorder she identified in 1974 after a study of 146 rape victims in Boston.

The first drawing, titled "Part 1" by Betty, shows her performing fellatio on Bryant Grober while an audience of stick figures watches the act. The second, third, and fourth drawings are Betty's depictions of being penetrated with bat, broom, and dowel stick on the Scherzer's couch. The last drawing contains two images: two male figures sucking Betty's exposed breasts and Betty touching a male's genitals.

As the pictures were shown to the jury, Dr. Burgess testified that the solid shaded renditions of the sex acts—in contrast to the simple line contours shown in the other parts of the drawings—indicate the intensity of Betty's feelings about the rape.

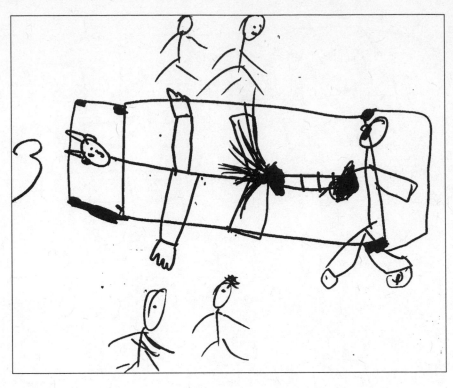

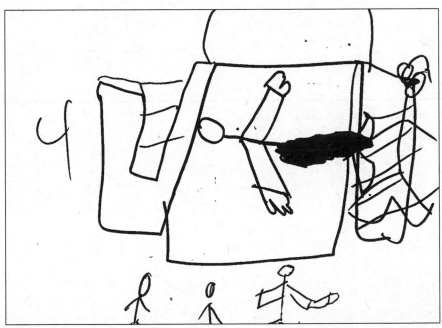

"Kyle had the stick," she said, and she described his giving it to Richie Corcoran, who announced that there was no need to lubricate it, and then, she said, "He stuck it up my vagina."

"And Betty," asked Laurino, "take a look at the stick that you talked to us about before, S-55, is that the stick?"

"Yes, it is," she said.

The sordid tale continued as Betty testified about further acts she performed that day. They wanted "blow-jobs," she said, and "they wanted to suck my tits—boobs."

"And did anybody suck on your boobs?" asked Laurino.

"Yes," she said.

Betty Harris had been on the witness stand over an hour. Her voice was often quiet; she looked exhausted. She was hungry. Judge Cohen recessed the trial for a short break reminding the jury, "Please don't discuss the case."

■

When the recess ended, Betty told the court that in her earlier testimony she confused the order of some of the events in the basement and some of the sex acts that took place that afternoon. The resulting exchange between witness, lawyers, and the judge was just one of many examples of bizarre courtroom theatrics as the case dragged on.

"Did anything happen just before they sucked on your boobs?" asked Laurino.

"Well," Betty started, "see… "

But Alan Zegas, the lawyer for Bryant Grober interrupted her. "I thought we went through a sequence before," he complained, "and she told us what they did before."

"I'm going to allow the question," ruled Judge Cohen, "although we have gone through the sequence." He turned to Betty and asked, "Is there anything that happened just before what you just mentioned?"

"Just before the sucking?" Betty asked the judge.

"Yes," he told her.

"I kind of messed it up a little," she realized.

"What is it that you kind of messed up a little?" asked the judge.

"See," she told him with her disarming honesty and straightforward manner of expressing herself, "I jerked them off, then I sucked them—their dicks—before I did it."

Chris Archer's lawyer spoke up. "What was that?" asked Thomas Ford. "She jerked them off?"

The judge asked the court reporter to read back Betty's last answer, and prosecutor Laurino continued, "Okay, Betty, when you say that you jerked them off, what did you do when you jerked somebody off. What does that mean?"

"What does that mean? It means that you put your hand on their dick and you go up and down."

Her telling of the story almost over, Betty still had to face cross-examination from the defense lawyers. Periodically she looked to the front row, to the spectator section where her sister and her friend Jennifer Lipinski smiled encouragement.

"Nothing else, nothing else," Betty said when asked what happened to her next. Kyle, she said, took the plastic bags off the bat and broom and washed the implements.

"How did you know it was then time to go, Betty?" asked Laurino.

"It wasn't time to go yet," she answered.

"What happened then before it's time to go? Does anybody say anything?"

"Not to tell anybody."

"Who says that?" he asks.

"All of them, all of them said that."

"Did they say what would happen if you told anybody?" Laurino wanted to know.

"They said that if I told anybody I'd get in trouble."

"Did they say what kind of trouble you'd get into?"

They were specific about the trouble, she said: "They'd tell my mother." That threat still concerned Betty. She told prosecutors she would tell her story in open court only if guaranteed that her parents would not attend the proceedings. Betty never shared her story of what happened in the Scherzer basement with them.

The threat to tell Betty's parents was combined with a vow of secrecy among the boys. They all gathered in a circle, placed their open palms one atop another and promised not to talk.

"I waited around to see if I would go out with Paul," Betty said, explaining what happened next. "Then Kyle said I could go home."

Laurino asked why she waited for Paul.

"Because I thought he still might want to go out with me."

"Did Paul go out with you that night?" she was asked.

"No," was the sad, simple answer, and her voice again was barely audible as she answered his next inquiry.

"Had Paul ever gone out with you before?"

"No."

And why did she not leave until Kyle ushered her out? Why did she stay through all the abuse?

" 'Cause I thought they weren't through with what they were doing."

Betty went to her friend Jennifer Lipinski's house next. She wanted to talk about what happened to her in the Scherzer basement, convinced Jennifer would keep the needed secret. But Jennifer was not home.

"The next day," asked Laurino, "when this was all done, the next day, could you tell us how you felt the next day?"

Betty's hands went up to her face, hiding it. "That's an embarrassing question."

Laurino tried again, and again Betty dodged: "It's embarrassing."

"I know it's embarrassing," he encouraged her. His voice was soft, and he coaxed her slowly, saying, "We're all grown-ups, so you can tell us, how did you feel, how did your body feel the next day?"

"It hurt," she finally said. "It hurt when I went to the bathroom." She let out a long, slow breath.

Before Laurino finished his questioning, after Betty identified her attackers, he asked, "Are those boys still your friends, the four boys?"

"Sort of," said Betty.

"What do you mean, sort of?" he asked.

"I mean I still care about them."

11.

Betty Faces Cross-Examination

The trial resumed the next morning with Betty back on the stand for cross-examination. "You can't handle her," worried Chris Archer's lawyer, Thomas Ford, the night before he started his questioning. He was referring to Betty's retardation. "I would love to have a Phi Beta Kappa graduate of Wellesley on the stand, someone that's very intelligent."

Ford approached Betty directly, immediately going to the heart of the case, by reminding her that she had testified that his client was a friend. "As a matter of fact, you still consider yourself a friend of Chris's, is that correct?"

"Yes," said Betty.

"And as you think back, Chris never did anything to hurt you, did he?"

"Yes, he did," said Betty firmly.

Ford, his strategy already failing, asked her to explain.

"He did the bat," was her straightforward reply.

His comeback line was a weak, "Well, is that the only thing that he ever did as far as you know that hurt you?"

"Yes," said Betty.

Despite his quick setback, Ford struggled vainly to elicit a response from Betty that would prove she was a willing participant in the basement acts. "You never told Chris that you didn't want him to touch you with the bat, did you?"

Betty looked puzzled. Judge Cohen asked her if she understood the question.

"No," she said.

"Please rephrase it," the judge asked the lawyer.

"All right," Ford agreed. "You never told anybody when you were in that cellar not to touch you?" he asked.

Betty was still confused. She hesitated, eventually saying, "That's a tough question."

Ford changed directions, reminding Betty about her testimony that Chris sucked her breasts. "You weren't forced?" Ford asked.

"Yes I was," insisted Betty. Just as he feared the night before, it was difficult for Ford to pursue Betty using traditional courtroom terminology and strategy.

"You are saying it is true that your breasts were sucked?" he asked.

"Yes."

"But nobody forced them, in other words, it wasn't done by somebody threatening you?"

"No, they just did it."

"In other words"—Ford tried to influence Betty—"nobody threatened you at all in that basement in March, did they?"

She thought about the question, a quizzical look on her face. "What do you mean by that?" she finally asked back.

"Well," said Ford, "nobody said, 'we're going to—you have to do this or you have to do this or we're going to do something to you if you don't do it'?"

Betty disagreed. "They said they were going to tell my mother."

But Ford reminded her, "That was after it was done, though."

And she agreed. "Yeah."

She agreed again as Ford tried to refute her testimony about feeling pain after the attack.

"You never complained about this problem to anyone, did you?" he demanded.

"No," she said.

"You didn't say anything to the doctor about this problem, did you?"

"No."

"You didn't take any medication, did you, after this?"

"No."

"There wasn't any bleeding or marks that you were aware of?" he asked.

"No marks," she said.

"And no bleeding?" he continued.

"No."

Repeatedly, Ford tried to establish that Betty was not forced by the gang. "What was it that caused you to take your clothes off?" he asked.

"They asked me to," was her simple answer.

"Who did?"

"Most of the kids, the guys."

Ford asked her about masturbating herself. "Did you then finger yourself?"

"They asked me to," she said.

"Did you do it?" he asked.

"Yeah," she acknowledged.

"Before you did that," he wanted to know, "did you say, I don't want to do it?"

"No," she testified.

Ford continued with questions, asking specifically and in detail about what happened when. At times Betty became confused and apologized. "It's all right," said Ford at one point, and he started his litany again with another crucial question. "Did you make any attempt to leave?"

"No way," Betty told him.

"No way," Ford repeated and asked, "You didn't make any attempt, you wanted to stay?"

"Yeah," said Betty.

"You knew if you wanted to get up and leave you could have?"

"Right," said Betty.

"No one was holding you from leaving?" he asked.

"Right," she said again.

"No one told you not to leave?" He kept at her.

"Correct," she said.

Before the rape began, as the boys were assembling, arranging the auditorium, seating Betty on the couch, the telephone rang upstairs. Kevin and Kyle Scherzer's grandmother answered the phone. It was for Kyle. The grandmother came about halfway down the stairs into the basement to fetch Kyle, who disappeared for a few minutes to talk. The grandmother returned to the main floor and remained out of the basement for the duration of the crime, apparently unaware of the bizarre activities taking place underneath her.

"You certainly wouldn't have fingered yourself if Kevin's grandmother were there, would you?" asked Ford.

"No."

"And you wouldn't have done any of the other things that happened if Kevin's mother were present, would you?"

"No," again.

"In other words, you would only do that in front of these boys?" he asked.

"Yes, sir."

"You wouldn't have done this in front of your parents?"

Betty's answer was without hesitation and firm. "Oh, no way."

"You wouldn't have done this in front of any adults?"

"Uh-uh," she said negatively.

"Because you knew they wouldn't like it?"

"Right."

After reiterating Betty's testimony about the broom and the bat, Ford tried again. "You knew you had the right to say, no, don't do it?"

"Yeah, I guess so," said Betty.

"You said no to people before who wanted to do things to you, didn't you?" asked Ford.

"No," answered Betty.

"You never said no to anyone?" he asked.

"Right," she said.

"No matter what anybody said, you always said yes?" he asked one more time.

"Yes," she said, bolstering the prosecutor's position again.

So Ford tried another tactic. He lit a match close to Betty's face. She reeled back in surprise. In earlier testimony, prosecution psychologist Dr. Susan Esquilin suggested Betty was so anxious to make friends and was manipulated so easily because of her mental handicap, she might allow herself to be physically burned in exchange for peer acceptance. Ford held the burning match. "Do you know what happens if you touch the burning end?" he asked Betty.

"No."

"You get burned?" he suggested.

"Oh, yeah," she agreed. "Yes, burned."

"You wouldn't let anybody burn you with a match would you?"

"No."

"You are too smart for that."

"Yeah."

"And you wouldn't let anybody stick you with a pin, would you?"

"No."

"If somebody burned you with a match, they wouldn't be your friend, would they?" he asked her.

Betty answered no, with a long drawn-out vowel sound. "Nooooo," she said, that now familiar childlike, singsong voice again reminding the jurors, the judge, the reporters, and all the spectators of her limited mental capacity.

Betty's deficiencies were perpetually obvious as she testified. The words and sentence structures of an eight-year-old kept coming out of her twenty-one-year-old mouth. Sometimes she would appear almost sweetly innocent, as just before a recess in the proceedings when Judge Cohen said to her, "Betty, we're going to break for lunch now. Please don't talk to anybody about the case."

"I'm not." she assured him. "I wouldn't."

"Good, thank you," he said.

But she wasn't finished. "I've been very good," she told the judge.

"Good," he said back to her. "Thank you."

"You are welcome."

Other times she sounded prepubescent, as when she was being

questioned about whether or not her mother knew she had offered to perform fellatio on classmates at Columbia High School. "No," she said, "until somebody opened their big mouth." Similarly, as Ford tried to guide Betty through an explanation of the time in her music class when she raised her blouse, he asked if her actions were of a "sexual nature." Betty looked at him, puzzled; she screwed up her face and asked, "What does that mean?" Yet the prior questions dealt with sexual intercourse; she testified she was "making out" with a boy at Columbia High School, "having sex."

■

"Good afternoon," Bryant Grober's lawyer, Alan Zegas, greeted Betty. "Hi," she responded.

Zegas asked Betty if she knew his client's name. "Grover," she said, mistaking the *b* for a *v* sound.

"Like in the Sesame Street character?" suggested Zegas.

Again Betty sang out, "Nooooo."

After a few questions, Betty seemed tired. It was 2:30 in the afternoon and the defense lawyers suggested a break, pointing out that the Ritalin Betty was taking to lengthen and focus her attention span wore off in early afternoon. The next morning Betty was up on the witness stand for a third day, seemingly refreshed.

"Good morning, Betty," said Zegas.

"Morning," she said.

"How are you?" he inquired.

"Fine." She was chipper. "Nice tie."

"Thank you," he said, and then launched into his questions. "You know an awful lot about sex, don't you?"

"Yes, I do," she agreed.

"And you've had a lot of experience with sex, haven't you?" he asked next.

"Yeah, I have."

"And that experience goes way back to your childhood, right?"

"Yes."

"And you would brag about your experience with sex, right?"

"Yup."

"Is there anything wrong," Zegas asked, "with being involved with sex with somebody else?"

"No," said Betty, "there's nothing wrong." Then she added, "It's a good thing."

"And it gives you a lot of good feelings?"

"Yeah."

"And it makes you happy?"

"Yeah."

"And it also makes the other person happy, right?"

"Oh sure, yeah."

"That makes you feel good about yourself?" It was phrased as a question.

"Uh-huh." The answer was affirmative.

"And it also makes the other person feel good, right?"

"Yeah."

"And isn't that the way a lot of times that you made other people feel good was to have sex with them?"

"Yeah."

"And there are a lot of boys you would approach and say that you would have sex with so that you would be happy and they would be happy, right?"

"Yup."

"And you would be the one to ask for sex, right?"

"Once in a while they asked," she said. "Sometimes I would."

"And when you said those kinds of things to boys, a lot of times that would get them excited, right?"

"Oh, yeah."

"And you knew that?"

"Uh-huh," again positively.

"And that made them feel good?"

"Definitely."

"And it made you feel good?"

"Yeah."

"And you enjoyed it?"

"Yeah."

"And you certainly would never tell your parents about that, right?"

"No way, José."

"You know that if you rub a boy's crotch, that's going to make him excited, right?"

"Yeah."

"It will make him happy?"

"Yeah."

"And sex can be a turn-on also for young women your age as well?"

"Oh, yes, even younger."

"About how young?"

"Twelve."

"And since the age of twelve, you've had these very strong feelings, haven't you, about sex?"

"Yes, I have," Betty told him.

"And the boys that you know, since the age of twelve, have also had very strong feelings about sex?"

"Yeah."

"And nothing's wrong with those feelings?" asked Zegas.

"No," Betty told him, "of course not."

"Do you know that when you give a boy a blow-job, and excuse the expression... "

"That's okay," Betty interrupted, dismissing his concern about terminology.

"You know when you give a boy a blow-job," he repeated, "that's something that can make him real happy, right?"

"Yeah, I know."

"You have a good feeling doing that, right?"

"Uh-huh."

"And you have a good feeling because you are close to the boy, is that right?"

"Yes."

"And the boy has a good feeling because he's close to you?"

"Yup."

Now Zegas moved to try to prove directly that his client did no wrong.

"You told Mari Carmen Ferraez that you loved giving a blow-job to Bryant Grober, right?"

"Yeah, I did say that, yes."

"And you told her it was exciting?"

"Yeah," said Betty.

"And there was a lot of excitement in your voice when you said it, right?"

"Uh-huh," she confirmed.

"It's because you really did feel excited by it?"

"Yeah."

"And it's something you wanted to do?"

"Uh-huh."

"And it's something you felt good doing?"

"Yeah."

"And it made him feel good as well?"

"Uh-huh."

"Now," said Zegas, as he strove to prove that Grober exerted no force against Betty, "you also know from your experience that if you are too rough with a boy on his penis, that could be painful to him, right?"

"Oh, yeah," said Betty, "you don't want to yank on it too much."

"And also," said Zegas, "a boy's balls are also very delicate, right?"

"Yeah," she said, "they're the size of a football field."

"If you unravel the tissues, you are saying?" Zegas sought clarification.

"Uh-huh."

"It would be the size of a football field because there's a lot of tissue inside the sac?"

"Yeah."

"But that area of the boy's body is a very soft delicate area, right?"

"Uh-huh."

"Okay, I want you to think back real carefully, Betty, to March first, okay, when you went to the park?"

"Okay."

"You went over to Bryant and you put your hand right up to his crotch and you said, 'Nice package you have there.' Do you remember that?"

"Yeah, I said that."

"And then did you say something like, 'Would you like me to suck on it?' Do you remember saying something like that or 'Would you like a blow-job?'—something like that? Think real carefully, okay, real carefully."

"Yeah. I guess I did say that, yeah."

"You remember saying that," Zegas affirmed. "Then after leaving Carteret Field and going into the Scherzers' basement, do you remember sitting on the couch next to Bryant at some point?"

"Uh-huh," said Betty.

"Do you remember being on the couch next to Bryant, and you reached over, and you rubbed his crotch, you rubbed his penis?"

Again she said, "Yeah, I did that, yeah."

"And that's how you started with him, right?"

"Yeah."

"You began to rub his penis?"

"Well," said Betty, "you mean…"

Zegas chose the vernacular. "His dick?" he asked.

"Yeah."

"You rubbed his dick?"

"Yeah."

"He didn't tell you to rub his dick, right, this is something you wanted to do?"

"Yeah."

"And after you began rubbing his dick you then asked him if he wanted a blow-job, right?"

"No," Betty finally disagreed. "He asked me if I wanted to give him a blow-job."

But Zegas retraced events with her, reminded her that she admitted trying to excite Grober. "And then eventually you did get him excited, right, and then you gave him a blow-job, which is what you wanted to do, is that right?"

"Yeah," said Betty.

"And then at some point while you were giving him a blow-job, your teeth touched his balls, is that right?"

"Yes, yes."

"And then he stood up, is that right?" asked Zegas.

"No." She contested his version, saying, "He couldn't have stood up. How could he stand up if my mouth is still on?..."

Zegas interrupted when she hesitated and tried to construct questions to show that rather than forcing Betty's head, Grober was in pain and was trying to guide Betty's consensual movements toward causing him pleasure instead of discomfort.

"Oh, God," responded Betty.

"Helping you make the blow-job feel better for him?" Zegas continued.

"I don't know," was Betty's response. "That's a tough question. I don't know."

"Do you remember being pretty strong on him with your mouth, do you know what I mean?"

"Oh, strong like… " Again the hesitation.

"Like sucking hard?" offered Zegas.

"No," she told him, "I wouldn't have sucked hard, no. You got to be easy, you know. No, no, no, I was easy with him."

"He seemed to like it?"

"Yeah."

"And you seemed to like it?"

"Yeah."

"And you did like it?"

"Yeah."

"You never said to him, Bryant, I hate what I'm doing?"

"No," she said.

"He wasn't forcing you to do what you were doing, right?"

"No."

"This is something you were doing because you, Betty, enjoyed it?"

"Yeah."

"Like you enjoyed it before with others, right?"

"Uh-huh, lots of people, yeah."

"You said the other day you don't know where Bryant Grober lives, do you?"

"No," said Betty, "no clue."

"And he's never been mean to you, has he?"

"No way," she agreed, adding, "he's a sweetheart."

"And he's never teased you or anything like that?"

"No, he's a sweetheart."

Alan Zegas was finished with Betty Harris.

■

Kevin Scherzer's lawyer, Michael Querques, the lawyer now famous for dismissing his client's role in the Glen Ridge affair with the simple "boys-will-be-boys" remark, took his turn at cross-examination.

"Betty"—he was ingratiating, speaking quietly—"can you tell I'm nervous?"

She was perceptive. "You don't look it," she told him.

He continued with the same tactic. "I'm a little afraid to ask you some questions."

"Don't be afraid," she counseled sweetly.

"Let me show you why I'm afraid," said Querques.

"You don't look it," Betty told him again.

"I know I don't look it, you just can't see it inside," he said. "Let me prove it to you."

Querques pointed out the three prosecutors with whom Betty worked preparing her testimony prior to the trial, and she agreed with him that they were her friends. "I'm not your friend, is that correct?" he lamented.

The question confused her. "What?" she said.

"We are not friends, you and I, are we?"

Betty reminded him, "I don't even know you."

When Thomas Ford questioned Betty, he spoke with her as if her mental capabilities were normal. Alan Zegas too used mostly traditional courtroom language as he got her to admit that she knew how to lie and kept secrets about sex from her parents and as he drew attention to the hours the prosecution rehearsed with Betty. Michael Querques took another tack.

"You think, Betty," he cooed, "do you think if I ask you pretty please, pretty please, Betty you'll try to be my friend for a couple of hours today and tomorrow?"

"Yes"—a typical monosyllabic answer from Betty.

"Now, you know if you are my friend you are supposed to tell me the gospel truth, don't you?"

"Yeah," she said, "that stupid Bible over there. Yup."

"This is a case," Querques said to her. "You know that Betty?"

"Oh sure, yeah."

"Some people told you this is the good side"—Querques pointed out the prosecutors' table—"and that's the bad side"—he identified the defense table. "Is that what you think, Betty, that's what you think, that's what they told you?"

"Uh-huh."

"Betty"—he went after her—"be real nice to me, Betty."

"Okay."

"Betty, who told you that side is the bad side?"

"Them," she said, pointing to Robert Laurino and the prosecutors' table.

"These are the same people, Betty," said Querques, "that brought you in on a Saturday and Sundays, the weekends, is that correct?"

"Uh-huh."

"Is that when you normally might shoot baskets?"

"Yeah."

"Is that when you normally might visit your friends, the Lipinskis?"

"Yes."

"Is that when you might go for ice cream, ride your bike, do something that you like to do?"

"I haven't been able to do that, but yes."

"You haven't been able to do that because they told you not to?"

"No, my parents did."

"Do you know if your parents told you because they told your parents, Betty?"

"No, I don't think so." She thought for a moment and asked, "You mean to ride my bike?"

"Yeah," said Querques as he tried to undermine Betty's favorable relationship with the prosecution, "ride your bike and go around town like you used to, Betty, they stopped it, didn't they, Betty?"

"Yeah," she agreed, "I hate them for that."

As Querques led Betty through a variety of questions, her mental limitations were made abundantly clear, over and over again.

"Some people think it's a dirty word to talk about sex," Querques announced. "Why?" asked Betty.

Later Querques mentioned one of the doctors who examined Betty: "We're going back, and we're going to pay him a visit." She misunderstood the figurative nature of his remark. "Why," she asked, "is he coming here?"

At another point, Querques pointed out Thomas Ford, saying, "This old guy, he's Tom Ford...." She interrupted with, "Does he drive a Ford?" "Hey, Betty," Querques informed her, "he drives a Jag!" "A Jaguar?" she asked back. "But his name is Ford."

When Querques identified the psychologist, Dr. Susan Esquilin, Betty said, "I hate that woman."

"You hate that woman?" Querques was pleased. "I'm glad you said it, Betty. Betty, excuse me, I shouldn't say that."

"That's all right," she comforted him.

"That's not nice for me to say.

"Why? It's how you feel."

"I'm sorry, Betty, I have to ask you why you hate that lady. What did she do?"

"She does things crazy," said Betty. "You know, the way she tests you and stuff."

"So you think she's a little..." Querques stopped.

"Wacky," Betty described her.

"You know," Querques told her, "it's funny, you must have read my mind, Betty, because I don't like to say crazy. I like to say wacky. So she's a little crazy or wacky?"

"Uh-huh."

"Now, Betty, I don't want to say it. Betty, I want to see if you say it. Do you say that this Dr. Susan Esquilin was on your back some-times?"

"Uh-huh."

"She was on your back, she was annoying you, Betty?"

"Oh, she was a pain in the butt."

"A lot of people in this case were on your back, weren't they?" Querques coached.

"Yeah."

"But isn't it odd, isn't it odd Betty, nobody from this side has been on your back?"

"Right."

"Until you came in here the other day, now we've been on your back a little bit, right?"

"Not really," she said.

"Not really," he repeated, "I love that. I appreciate that. We haven't been on your back. I appreciate that."

"You are doing the best you can." Betty again comforted him, adding, "that's all that counts."

"Oh, you are wonderful, Betty. You are wonderful, Betty."

"Okay."

"Some people, not me, Betty, some people say that you are retarded. Now, that's not true, is it Betty?"

"Well," she reflected, "a lot of people used to call me that in school."

"But you don't believe that, do you Betty?"

"No," she answered. "I don't look retarded."

"And you are proving to these people right now, because you can answer questions, that you are not retarded?"

"Right. If I was retarded, I couldn't answer these questions. I wouldn't know what I'm talking about."

"Perfect, Betty," gloated Querques.

In fact, Querques's ingratiating line of questioning and her simplistic and naive answers reinforced the belief in jurors' minds that Betty was unable to say no.

■

As the day of cross-examination ended, Querques called Kevin Scherzer from his chair on the defense side of the courtroom and positioned his client directly in front of Betty.

"Betty," he said to her, "who is this big guy, Betty?"

"Oh, he's a body builder."

"What's his name, Betty?"

"Kyle." She mistook him for his twin brother, but quickly corrected herself. "No, Kevin."

"Now you don't want to hurt him, do you?" asked Querques.

"No," she said. "I don't want to see anybody hurt."

"You don't want to hurt anybody?" he asked again.

"Right," she explained. "I care about them. I know they don't give a hoot about me, but I care about them."

Querques tried to change her mind. "He was always considerate of you, wasn't he?"

She started to agree, saying, "Yeah, he always…," but she hesitated. Betty knew otherwise, and she finished her answer with, "He never spent much time with me because he was always busy with his other friends."

"You like him, don't you?" Querques prodded.

"Yes," she said about the body-building, six-foot-tall football hero, "he's very handsome."

"You more than like him," Querques encouraged.

"Yes."

"You love him a little bit."

"Uh-huh."

"Maybe a lot?"

"A lot," said Betty, "yes."

■

After three days on the witness stand, the ordeal of testifying in open court was almost over for Betty. The next morning, December 16, 1992, nearly four years after the rape, Louis Esposito, the lawyer for Kyle Scherzer, dismissed Betty with a surprising announcement. "I'm not going to ask you any questions," he said. "I'm going to wish you a happy Christmas from myself and Mr. Kyle Scherzer."

The next day Betty was back on the stand, remembering the "sweetheart" of the day before, Bryant Grober, without the fondness she had expressed to the defense lawyers. She stumbled through a litany of questions from prosecutor Laurino and changed her story to a claim that the act of fellatio was forced on her. Of more importance to the case than her recanting of her previous testimony that she enjoyed the act and that it was voluntary, was the confusion she expressed on the stand. Her hesitation, her gestures covering her eyes and mouth, and her simplistic interpretation of what the trial was all about helped the prosecution prove that her mental faculties were simply not adequate to give consent to the sex foisted on her by her neighbors. Betty's final testimony was reminiscent of her reaction, days after the rape, when she pleaded to her swimming teacher, "How do I say no?"

As Laurino requestioned Betty, he reminded her that the day before she had called Grober a "sweetheart." She told him "it wasn't true," that Grober was no such thing, and "I'm going to be honest now."

Laurino next tried to extract from Betty why Grober was not a sweetheart. "He never cared about me," was her response.

Laurino wanted to know if it was a strain for Betty to tell her story in front of the four defendants, the neighbors she said she still considered friends.

Her hesitation started, and she struggled to voice her answer, eventually coming out with, "To some extent," adding that she felt "confused."

Laurino wanted a further explanation, and the best she managed was to say, "Because here's one side and here's the other side. It's hard to choose between one side and the other." With her eyes she made it clear as she spoke that she was referring to the prosecution and the defense. Obviously Querques's questioning about good guys and bad guys the day before had confused her.

As Laurino pushed for more details, her hesitation returned. Judge Cohen intervened and asked Laurino's question again. Was it difficult for her to testify in front of the defendants? Her voice faltered as she answered, "I was concerned."

Laurino asked for an explanation of the answer.

After more hesitation, her voice was quiet as she told him, "That's a hard question to answer." Her hands went to hide her head, and the judge asked her if she knew the answer. Her head shook.

The questions ended.

■

Betty Harris, now a piece of American crime folklore and legal history, left the courtroom. But the case would not remain behind her. In addition to her memories of the Scherzer basement, she had the appeal process to wait through. Next on her schedule was some sort of vocational training, as her parents tried to prepare her for adult life. She continued to live in the same neighborhood with the rapists, but she expressed no concern for her safety. As her testimony indicated, she still looked at the four of them as friends. Her retardation seemed to have saved her from feeling the ongoing fear and paranoia suffered by many rape victims long after the crime against them is adjudicated.

12.

Paul Archer's Lies

After the prosecution rested its case, the defense lawyers brought Paul Archer before the jury, expecting to seal their case with his eyewitness account. "She was fine." Christopher Archer's brother tried to assure the jury about Betty Harris. "She asked us to come back a second day to do it again. She enjoyed it," Archer said with arrogant self-assurance. "She said she enjoyed it," he repeated, identifying Betty as "voluntarily doing everything."

Archer initially described Betty as a skillful seductress, an experienced participant orchestrating the antics of the thirteen boys surrounding her in the basement. "She was totally in control," Paul Archer testified. "She made all the advances. She was the one doing everything. It was all her idea."

Paul Archer was lying.

A year before, when he pleaded guilty to endangering the welfare of an incompetent person, he testified that Christopher Archer and Kevin Scherzer "put" the broom into Betty. But now, on the witness stand, he was changing his plea-bargain story, claiming not only that it was Betty who called for the broom, but that "she asked for something bigger and Kevin got the baseball bat."

The next day Archer was back on the stand, changing his story again, adding contradictory details, saying Kevin Scherzer pushed the broomstick once it was inside Betty while she "moaned with pleasure." The day before he limited Kevin Scherzer's activities to holding the broomstick.

Michael Querques tried to lead Archer safely through his story.

"Your friend Kevin over there"—Querques pointed out Scherzer —"What did he do?"

"He held on to the opposite end of the broom," was Archer's answer.

"Tell me why," said Querques.

Archer said he could offer no explanation.

So Querques suggested Scherzer was "assisting" Betty.

"Yes," Archer agreed.

Querques asked if Scherzer "pushed" the broom.

"Yes," again from Archer, "after she inserted it."

Prosecutor Glenn Goldberg seized on the changing story. "Have you told us any lies in court?" he demanded.

"No, I haven't," said Archer, explaining that he had said his brother and Scherzer "put" the broom into Betty because "I was nervous and I wasn't thinking."

His third day on the stand, Archer admitted that back when police first asked him about the crime, he lied to investigators in an attempt to protect his gang. "I was nervous," he said about his interviews with detectives several weeks after the attack. "I just didn't want to tell anything. I was trying to evade any involvement. I wanted to evade any involvement of my friends."

And Archer contradicted his testimony of only days before, saying Betty "had help" when she was penetrated by the bat and the broomstick, that Kevin Scherzer, Betty, and the broom "were going along together" for a few minutes.

The defense's star witness was falling apart.

Before he finished his testimony, Paul Archer acknowledged committing a moral error. "Yes, I did think it was wrong in a moral sense," he agreed with Goldberg, "because there was a girl performing sexual acts on herself and we stood around and watched." Archer admitted that Betty was provided with the broom and bat, even though he was emphatic in repeating that "she was the one who wanted to do it. She was the one who initiated everything. She was the one asking to do things. She was the one in control."

Yet when Goldberg asked Archer if Betty asked for help before the broom was pushed, he answered, "No, she didn't."

Goldberg sought an explanation for the motive of the crime. Why did he watch an act he now called morally wrong, an act he did not try to stop? the prosecutor asked Archer.

"Just curious," was the answer, followed by, "I don't know."

Bryant Grober's lawyer, Alan Zegas, led Archer through a series of questions in an attempt to resolve why the group tried to keep the incident a secret. "I didn't want my mother or teachers to find out," said Archer. "I didn't want my parents to know I observed a girl performing sexual acts. It's embarrassing. I thought it was morally wrong. But I didn't think we had committed any legal wrong."

After the jury pronounced the four men guilty, Christopher Archer's lawyer, Thomas Ford, looked back on Paul Archer's testimony—the only eyewitness testimony besides Betty's—as a severe error in defense tactics. "From my point of view," he said, "we'd have been better off not having Paul Archer." It was Bryant Grober's lawyer who wanted Archer to testify because Archer confirmed that Grober separated himself from the crowd before the broom and bat were deployed.

"I would never have called him," Ford said about Archer. "I didn't want him. If he didn't testify, there would have been nobody to buttress and support the testimony," he said of Betty's story. "Obviously, it was the bat and broom that upset the jury. Without that buttressing, there may have been some question as to just what occurred. In a case like this, you don't put anyone on to buttress her."

Juror Patrick Parker, a truck driver, talked to reporters in detail after the trial about the case and the jury's deliberations. He agreed with Ford that putting Paul Archer on the stand was a serious mistake for the defense. "His brother is on trial. He is interested in one thing, and that is to get his brother off." Expecting the jury to believe Archer, said Parker, is "like saying we are stupid."

The
Verdict

13

I t wasn't their desire to get the truth, unfettered, unvarnished, before you," Thomas Ford complained to the jury about the prosecutors' case as he summed up his arguments for acquittal. "It's almost as if the state is trying to present one of those show trials—the way they did in Russia under Stalin." Ford repeatedly insisted to the jury that Betty Harris knew what she was doing in the basement and wanted to do it. "She didn't say, 'I didn't have any choice.' She knew deep in her own mind, in her own heart, that everything that occurred there was something she willingly participated in." The activities in that basement, said Ford, were not rape; they were consensual sex. "She took the broom in her own hands and inserted it, and when she finished that the bat came along, and she took the thick end and held it and tried but was unsuccessful." The boys in the basement were not rapists, his message insisted; they were just helping.

Nonsense, responded prosecutor Glenn Goldberg in his closing speech. He attacked Michael Querques's "boys-will-be-boys" defense. "Boys may experiment with bugs and frogs and laboratory rats," he said with disgust, "but they don't experiment with human females' bodies. This is no prank. You cannot commit a prank on a young woman with a bat and a broomstick." He hammered away at Querques. "Boys play ball with bats. Boys sweep floors with brooms.

Boys are not permitted to put household cleaning utensils inside girls." He rejected Querques's characterization of Betty Harris as an example of a girl who likes "to see the joy on a boy's face when he ejaculates" as proof that she sought out the basement assault. "A bat doesn't ejaculate. It's not going to bring joy and pleasure to a girl's face." Goldberg's summation continued for days. Toward the conclusion, after more than six days of speaking, he reiterated his basic case over and over again with graphic representations of the crime. "What she got was spread-eagled in a cramped little basement and raped with sticks wrapped in garbage bags and smeared with Vaseline. It was not an act of love. It was not even an act of sex. If it was performed on a helpless creature it would be considered inexcusable cruelty. This mentally defective girl was pathetically eager to please people. She paid an extraordinary price because of her extraordinary vulnerability. She can be taunted, teased, abused, poked, and prodded with sticks, but she matters and her life matters, too." After fourteen hours and fifteen minutes, Glenn Goldberg sat down, and the Glen Ridge rape case went to the jury.

■

"This is a criminal trial," Judge Cohen reminded the jurors as he instructed them in their duties before they began the deliberations that were to continue for several days, sometimes degenerating from balanced debate into screaming matches. "They are not on trial for allegedly teasing, they are not on trial for doing things that were not nice or foolish or may have even been immoral." Betty Harris "is not on trial here," the judge reminded the jurors.

The complex set of charges left the jurors with a wide variety of options if they decided to convict the defendants of a crime—from first-degree sexual assault to much lesser conspiracy charges. First, the jury needed to decide whether or not Betty was mentally defective, as defined by New Jersey law—that is, whether or not she was able to understand her right to refuse to engage in the activities in the basement and whether or not her mental abilities were adequate for her to exercise that right if, indeed, she understood it.

Quickly, the jurors agreed that Betty Harris was legally mentally defective. They also decided early on that the defendants knew, or at least should have known, that Betty was mentally defective. Then the deliberations bogged down, the days wore on, and the jury room became the scene of frustration and fights. Finally, after twelve days, the verdicts were decided. All four men were convicted of conspiracy to commit aggravated sexual assault and aggravated sexual contact. For Bryant Grober, the conspiracy verdict carried less weight. He was convicted of conspiracy in the third degree. For the other three it was second-degree conspiracy. Grober was convicted of nothing else. But Christopher Archer and Kevin Scherzer each were found guilty of first-degree aggravated sexual assault, specifically, penetration of a mentally defective person with a bat, a broom, and a dowel stick. Another first-degree assault verdict was levied against Archer and Kevin Scherzer for committing the assault using force or coercion. Kyle Scherzer was also found guilty of first-degree aggravated sexual assault with the use of force or coercion. His guilt on the other aggravated sexual assault charge was gauged by the jury to be a second degree offense.

All four defendants were acquitted of the other charges pending against them: forced fellatio, fellatio performed by a mentally defective person, the improper touching of Betty's breasts, and their forcing her to masturbate them. After the jury was dismissed, juror Mario Tolentino blamed the acquittals on Betty's lack of credibility: "She changed her testimony to try to please whoever the lawyer was who was asking the questions." Precisely the behavior that provided the jurors with the basis for judging Betty mentally defective prevented them from finding guilt on the other charges. Tolentino explained, "There was not enough evidence."

Judge Cohen read through the verdicts. The four rapists stood, no longer laughing and joking with their friends as they were through much of the jury's deliberations. They stood straight, their faces without expression. They left the court, followed by their families. Only Grober's father, physician Nathan Grober, responded to reporter's questions. "Enough," he said, "is enough."

But several of the jurors chose to share their feelings. Especially talkative was truck driver Patrick Parker. He identified the Mari Carmen Ferraez tapes as particularly helpful to his decision-making process, specifically when Ferraez asked Betty what she would do if she were approached anonymously on the street by a man asking for sex. "She said, 'I don't know,'" Parker recounted after the verdict was read. "That helped me. To me, that meant she couldn't come out and say, 'No.'"

The most difficult work for the jury was deciding whether or not the defendants knew Betty was mentally defective. "If they didn't know before the broom," he and the rest finally decided, "they had to know after the broom. No human being would submit to that, period."

Two months later, when Judge Cohen slapped the rapists on the wrists with his sentence and allowed them to stay at the Shore and in the bars, on no more than $2,500 bail, juror Parker expressed his depression and frustration. "What I feel I really can't even put into words. To me it felt like what we did was for nothing." Parker, along with so many other observers of the trial, speculated about racism and classism. Would the four of them be locked in prison were they black and poor? "I know the answer," said Parker. "Now I want to put it behind me. It's like the judge was telling us that the time we put in didn't matter. We wasted taxpayers' money, five months out of our lives. I felt from the beginning that maybe they would get off light. After the verdict, when the guys were not remanded for a first-degree offense, I thought, 'The judge wants to get them off.'"

Betty's Best Friend

14

Basketball and the neighborhood brought Betty together with Jennifer Lipinski. They met during high school, on the quiet streets along the Bloomfield-Glen Ridge border, Betty—in her typical style—smiling at Jennifer and offering a friendly hello. Soon, Betty looked to Jennifer as her best friend and to Jennifer's house—filled with brothers and sisters—as a second home. They shot baskets with each other. Betty was a frequent dinner guest at the Lipinski table. The girls went shopping together, ate ice cream, and talked.

"She's told me a lot," says Jennifer. "For some reason she took a liking to me. I just think because I was one of the few people her age that really was interested in what she had to say and really looked at her as more normal than anyone else did and as just a person. And she liked that."

Dusk is glowing on a sultry late spring evening soon after the sentencing of the rapists. Jennifer, now a basketball star and business major at the University of Delaware, is about to graduate and head off for a European tour before starting graduate school. We meet at the Deer Park Tavern, a noisy beer and nachos bar just off campus in Newark (Delaware, not New Jersey), where in 1913 organizers of the women's suffrage movement gathered to plot strategy. Now twenty-two years old, Jennifer is a vivacious, wide-eyed young woman. She needs no prompting or encouragement to talk about Betty and the case, which continues to be a dominant benchmark in her own life. She is angry that the convicted rapists remain free.

Dazed after the rape, Betty made her way out of the Scherzers' dank basement to the comforting confines of the Lipinski house. "She had come to tell me," Jennifer remembers. But, as was the case so often, Jennifer was not home. She played three different sports during high school, and it seemed she was always practicing. "She had come down to tell me and I wasn't home, so she went home."

A couple of days later, after Betty confided to her swimming teacher, she caught up with Jennifer. "She didn't even tell me the whole thing." Initially, Jennifer was unaware of the seriousness of the incident. "I didn't know exactly what was done, the fact that they used a baseball bat."

But the two were close enough that Jennifer could tell something was bothering Betty. "I'd say, 'Bett, what's wrong?' And she'd say, 'Nothing.'" This was a pattern Jennifer had seen before. If Betty wanted to share something that was troubling her, she would never bring it out directly, but Jennifer would notice a change in Betty's usually cheerful mood.

"She was definitely beating around the bush this time." Jennifer kept asking what was wrong, and Betty kept saying, "Never mind, never mind." Jennifer kept pressing, and finally Betty said, "They tricked me."

Jennifer asked, "Who tricked you?"

"All of them did," was Betty's response.

"Did you tell your mom?" Jennifer asked Betty, and Betty said she had not, but that the swimming teacher knew.

At first Betty would not name names, Jennifer tells me as she sips a beer. We're sitting outside, on the Deer Park's covered veranda. At the next table three coeds are laughing, drinking beers, trading stories about boys. Convertibles cruise by, guys wave, horns honk.

"I couldn't get that much out of her," Jennifer tells me about that first day. "If I had known what I know now, of course, I would have either called her mother or done something. That's one thing I really regret."

Jennifer speaks rapidly. She is intense and earnest, with a well-scrubbed all-American look, comfortable in her college-town element, comfortable in a blousy blue shirt and white shorts; silver rings and bracelets catch the fading light. She joins me in combing through her own Glen Ridge history for some understanding of the crime.

"I knew the Archers. They lived right by the park. They used to be there all the time. They were the ones who used to call her 'Piggy' and 'Pigorskiac.'" It was more than teasing, it was taunting. Jennifer tried to stop the name calling. "Betty sometimes used to laugh but didn't really. They were really making fun of her. We'd be shooting baskets. The Archers would be there, just kind of hanging around; it's not like they even came to play basketball. Once in a while, but they weren't basketball lovers or basketball athletes." They called out at Betty at the park, and they called her on the telephone and said, as Jennifer puts it, "nasty things."

Jennifer was the good friend who told the Archers to leave Betty alone, to stop the attacks, that it wasn't right. "Soon after that, if I was there, they didn't really bother her that much." But when Betty was at the park without her friend, the taunting continued, and Betty would bring the stories back to Jennifer.

"You look at Betty and it's evident that some kind of disability is there," Jennifer explains above the bar chatter, "and to just pick on her like that, to just call someone names—it wasn't like it was in fun, and they were her buddy, because that was not the case."

But at Jennifer's house, Betty did find buddies. "Betty is like family to us." Jennifer is searching out loud to understand why the Archers and the others abused her. "She had a good time with our family. I felt that I was doing so much for her, honestly, because she would actually listen to what I had to say and follow my advice." Jennifer tried to motivate Betty to study. "What I think she needed to hear more was that she was a bright person, and she had talents, and she just needed to work on them a little harder, maybe a little harder than everybody else, but that she was capable of doing a lot." And it worked. Jennifer saw evidence of her influence: Betty would study more after they talked.

But it was that same susceptibility to influence, figures Jennifer, that gave the rapists an opening; they recognized Betty's vulnerability to manipulation, how easy it would be to get her to do something. "I just felt that they were just bored one day, that they could get away with something like that because it was Betty." Jennifer is struggling, trying to comprehend the motivation, and she stumbles on the same line used by the defense, "You know—boys are boys. I mean they have—you know—sick minds I guess—I don't know—at that age. But I just think that they knew, or thought, that they could do something like that and get away with it."

I tell Jennifer that I am quite uncomfortable with the "boys-will-be-boys" characterization. We're surrounded by boys at the Deer Park Tavern, and we don't seem to be surrounded by rapists. Jennifer quickly agrees that her New Jersey friends who are boys could never perpetrate a crime such as the one committed against Betty. "Oh, no, no, no! That wasn't the element that I associated with at all. You have to be really demented to think of something like what they did and to go about it that way. I would like to get their opinion on that." She wants to know how they thought up the idea to assault Betty and what made them carry out the crime.

■

During the trial, Jennifer testified about what Betty told her a few days after the attack. "She said she went to the Scherzer basement. There was a little bat that was used. Vaseline was also used, and they stuck it up her. She said she was coerced into going down there and was forced into doing it." Jennifer's testimony was important, not to establish that a crime was committed, but to prove that Betty did complain about what the rapists did to her.

■

"When I left that stand," Jennifer is saying at the Deer Park, "I felt like I had really done something good. I felt really good about myself. My mom had passed away. She was very close with Betty also.

I knew she would have been so proud of me to get up there." The memory of that day makes Jennifer speak even faster. "Betty had to endure so much through this whole thing: social criticism, people passing judgment left and right. She's gone through a lot. She's already had to yield enough just by living with a disability in general. I felt awful. Just the fact that she doesn't have a license. She would love to have her license and just drive and stuff. She was so excited when she turned twenty-one because she said she went out and drank a beer. I don't think there's anything wrong with that. She can never really go out and have the freedom of being as independent as other people. And then for her to go through all of this. So I was happy, to say the least, that they were found guilty." And sad that Judge Cohen left them out on bail during the appeals process. "I was upset. Our judicial system—it's not all that it's cracked up to be, I think. It was just upsetting. I don't think they got what they deserved. That's such a heinous crime. Just the whole plot itself, just the planning of it, that a group of boys could actually sit down and think that up and then go through with it, that's demented." Jennifer is getting more and more upset. She cannot believe that the judge doesn't consider the rapists a further threat to society, that her friend's assailants now figure they were able to get away with the crime. Instead she wants them to sit in jail and think about what they did. "There's definitely psychological treatment that they have to undergo. And obviously it couldn't have happened to a nicer person and someone who deserves it less. Betty has a heart of gold, honestly. She would do anything for anyone." Jennifer quickly realizes that in the context of the events we've been discussing, her last remark could be misunderstood. "What I mean by that is just errands, or just help."

As we finish our beers, Jennifer Lipinski is still upset and forecasts more crimes like the one that damaged her friend—although at the time she was unaware of a carbon-copy rape that had already occurred a few months before in North Carolina. "Society is really hurt. Look at kids their age possibly looking at the penalties they received and then maybe not thinking twice before they themselves would do something to that effect. How could they not be a threat to society? They've just done so much damage. I don't understand the rationalization there, I really don't."

■

Jennifer is a true friend of Betty's. But Betty's mental impairment precludes her from making an adequate differentiation between someone who really cares for and about her, like Jennifer, and someone who is just out to use her. "Basically," prosecutor Robert Laurino concluded about Betty's understanding of friendship, "Betty's idea is that if you're a friend, whatever you ask of another friend, that friend should do, because friends do things for other friends. So whatever she was asked, she would do. So she did not see what happened to her as victimization. It was something she was asked to do, and since she was a friend, and since they said they were friends, she did it in response."

Betty's philosophy of friendship would work just fine if her encounters could be restricted to friends like Jennifer Lipinski.

Monday Morning Quarterbacking with Thomas Ford

15

Several miles through the New Jersey suburban sprawl from Glen Ridge is a drab two-story office building nestled amid shade trees, separated from Millburn Avenue by its asphalt parking lot. The building houses doctors and lawyers' offices, including that of Christopher Archer's lawyer, Thomas Ford. His foppish courtroom attire is in his closet the Saturday morning we sit down to discuss his notorious case. Ford's belly is pushing against a light blue Lacoste pullover, his Mont Blanc ball-point casually clipped between the open buttons. His blue slacks are checkered; his belt is white. The slight curl of his closely cropped hair, his matching silver bushy eyebrows, and his trim mustache conspire with his country club clothes to create a dandified weekend appearance.

"We were not totally unhappy with the sentencing." Ford clears his throat and quickly continues, not wanting to appear to agree with critics who say that his client's sentence was light. He offers a negative interpretation of Judge Cohen's decision: "Of course the young men got fifteen years, which means they could get out in around three—a little more, a little less, depending on the prison authorities." But Ford insists that he does not interpret the relatively light sentence as a victory.

"I feel that we should have won the case, based on the evidence that we presented," he says, looking across his cluttered desk. In contrast to his studied personal appearance, the office is a mess of documents. Piles of legal briefs and court transcripts litter the space. Ford's desk is in the middle of the room, full of paperwork. Cardboard file boxes are stacked in a corner. On the credenza is a little statue of a monkey. The monkey is dressed in a three-piece suit, sports a watch chain, a British-style jurist's wig, and half-spectacles, and is carrying a writ of habeas corpus.

A few months have passed since the trial ended. Ford is not handling Christopher Archer's appeal; the job is now in the hands of the public defender because the Archer family is out of money. "I think we lost," he says about the most publicized case of his career, "because we had a jury that was bitterly divided. They arrived at a compromise verdict after they were out over a week. I know there was a lot of rancor in the jury room because we heard pounding on the walls. As a matter of fact"—he drops the story into our conversation like a headline in the *National Enquirer*—"one of the young female jurors sent a note out asking that the bat be removed from the jury room because she was apprehensive that it might be used against her. She was apparently one of those that was holding out." Ford looks up to see if the anecdote intrigues me. He knows what makes a news story—he's been in the national limelight with the Glen Ridge case, and his son works for CNN. In fact, during the deliberations, one juror did yell at another, "I want that bat out of here. I don't trust you!"

Analyzing the verdict, Ford explains why it makes no sense to him. "There were nine counts in the indictment. Three of the boys [including his client, Archer] were convicted on three counts and acquitted on six. The six that they were acquitted on dealt with basically the same type of sexual acts based on the same type of testimony. Now how the jury could say they'll believe the girl on three counts and disbelieve her on others is beyond me."

But it isn't really beyond him. Ford is quick to keep talking, to offer his theory. Despite his son's occupation, despite Ford's hospitality to reporters, he places some blame for his loss on the extensive news coverage the case generated. He asserts that it is the notoriety of the case, and the involvement of objects such as the bat and broom, that affected the jury's decision. "In other words," he tries to make his point clear, "they said perhaps she could consent as to masturbating them or as to having them fondle her, but they just couldn't buy the fact that she would consent as to the broom and bat."

And with those words, Ford gets to the crux of the case in terms of its ghoulish popular appeal. No matter what legal technicalities may complicate the issues involved, for most lay observers of the Glen Ridge case, the broom and the bat represent nothing but rape.

"There was sympathy for the girl," Ford understands, but he suggests it was sympathy that improperly affected the jurors' interpretation of the facts. As an example, Ford points to the dramatic and graphic drawings of the rape that Betty made during therapy sessions. These, the judge ruled, were not to be considered direct evidence of the crime, but evidence of what occurred during Betty's meeting with the psychologist who was treating and studying her. "However, the jury specifically asked questions relative to the pictures. These pictures impressed them" as evidence of a crime, complains Ford, citing what he considers just one example of mistakes made during the trial.

No matter how complicated the details of the case, says Ford, the guilty verdict comes directly from the revulsion the jurors felt toward the use of the broom and the bat. "I think what the jury said is, 'We don't believe she—anybody—would consent to this. My argument was, many people do, many people have, many people will consent to abnormal sex acts." It was a position Ford could not persuade the jury to accept. "The combination of her mental state and the abnormality of the sex acts presented a problem to the jury, and I think that's what led to the conviction."

People choose to engage in all forms of sexual activity, says Ford, illustrating his point with legendary tales. "There are innumerable stories about women using Coke bottles, about people putting on shows on stages involving donkeys, which people go to and watch. Obviously, if people are watching it, somebody has to be doing it. I have never gone around trying to document it. I have never seen those shows, but I know from my experience over the years that they do exist."

As Ford interprets the events in the Scherzer basement, Betty was not necessarily seeking her own gratification, she was attempting to please her audience. "In other words, I've heard"—and, he quickly adds—"I've never been to any, I've heard stories about—ah—at bachelor parties where two women perform sexual acts on each other, and, I would presume, acts that would not physically damage them, people would do. In other words, if people would insert a finger, they could insert anything."

He points to the lack of physical damage to Betty as further evidence that no crime was committed. "A lot of people think when they see a bat or they see a broom that this was something like a bayonet—like they claim the Japanese did in Nanking. You have to realize," he says about what his client did, "that it wasn't that abberational in the sense that there was injury."

We return to the question of consent, specifically, whether Betty consented to the use of the broom and the bat. "You have to bear in mind," Ford insists, speaking slowly and quietly, "that basically she said she did. There's no testimony that anybody ever held her or forced her to act. The issue that the State made was that she wanted to please these boys, there were so many there, that this overbore her will." Ford remains unconvinced by such an argument. Neither, he says, was he convinced by his colleague Michael Querques's argument that the crime could be explained away because "boys will be boys." Calling himself morally straitlaced, Ford identifies the Querques defense as a failure, if only because there were so many women on the jury. "I don't believe boys should do it," he says about activities like the Scherzer basement spectacle. "I pointed out," Ford says about his opening arguments to the jury, "that what these boys did might have been morally reprehensible—it was something I would never have condoned—it was not something that I was telling the jury they should be lauded for; rather, I condemned it. But they did not commit a crime—that was the theory I used."

No longer in regular contact with Archer, Ford says he is sure that

Archer and the other rapists "didn't know her mental state to the point where they could say that she couldn't say yes or couldn't say no." Then, as he did during the trial, Ford turns for justification and explanation to Betty's promiscuity. "How many people are going to walk up to the football team in the cafeteria and offer to perform fellatio on all of them?"

Thomas Ford views his client not as a perpetrator of an evil crime, but as another victim. "I would say that this was a case that was permeated with victims. The parents of both sides were victims. Other members of the families were victims. Their friends and associates were victims. Betty, you can say if you want, was a victim both ways. She was a victim of what occurred, and the publicity changed all their lives. Yes, I think the case could have been disposed of in an entirely different fashion that would have suited the interest of both parties." A plea to a lesser offense—say, improper touching, criminal contact of some less severe degree—is his recommendation for a better resolution. He charges the prosecutors were the ones who wanted the high-profile trial, snidely saying, "Let me put it this way: What prosecutor doesn't benefit from publicity?" He quickly adds, "I'm not making an accusation. That happens in every case." He smiles.

■

The publicity surrounding the Glen Ridge case is enormous. While working on this book I mention the project to friends and colleagues, and find hardly anyone who was unaware of the crime. All I needed to say are three key things: New Jersey, four athletes, a retarded victim.

But the prosecutors laughed out loud when I tell them about Ford's suggestion that they used the case to further their own careers. "And here we are today!" Robert Laurino roars, pointing out the dilapidated offices of the Essex County prosecutors.

"It's classic how they perceive things." Elizabeth Miller-Hall mocks. "What's extraordinary is that you're working so hard on the case to do what's right, to do the best job that you can, that to some degree you're not even aware of all the press coverage that's occurring. When you've gotten a few hours of sleep at night and you have fought and argued and gone through all these different thoughts of how you're supposed to do something, the last thing you're aware of or thinking of is that you're on TV."

Glenn Goldberg smiles too, then turns serious. "That's a common theme of defense attorneys and defendants in any case in which they wish to come up with some alternate theory to take away the attention from the defendants' guilt," he says irritably, "that the prosecutors have some particular motive. I've had cases where it's been asserted that I have political desires or ambitions—governor, president, I don't know what. That's all nonsense. It's totally absurd."

There is no question, though, that the case brought attention to the three prosecutors. "We're doing the same things we always did," Miller-Hall points out months after the trial ended. "Nothing has changed."

GANG RAPE IN THE SUBURBS is *Newsweek*'s first headline about the case; DAY OF HORROR, the magazine calls the rape. ASSAULT CASE SHAKES AFFLUENT N.J. TOWN, says *USA Today*. THE SLOW GIRL AND THE JOCK KINGS is how the headline for Anna Quindlen's column sums up the equation in the *New York Times*. Even the defense lawyers become quasi celebrities. Michael Querques achieves infamy with his offensive "boys-will-be-boys" argument, and after the verdict, all four of the losers decorate the front page of the *New Jersey Law Journal* under the banner headline, THEY COULD HAVE DONE BETTER.

■

Thomas Ford leans back in the chair behind his desk. He looks across his office at an oil painting of a horse race. "They were all high school athletes, and they all came from one town." He tries to explain why the case attracted such attention, to debunk the charges that the boys were children of privilege gone wrong. "They weren't as affluent as they were made out to be. There was nothing to indicate, no testimony, not even a suggestion, that because they played football or baseball that they were treated any differently than anyone else. High school athletes are not heroes. These were very normal, ordinary type kids. It was blown out of proportion. In other words, it could very well be that there are cases like this, maybe more reprehensible, where people take a girl and hold her down and force her to have sex and injure her—you understand—and this wouldn't get any headlines at all."

As for himself, Ford "didn't mind the publicity," except for the drain on his time. "I never envisioned the trial taking six months. This totally enveloped me. I had to do other things, but it enveloped me. This was the only thing people wanted to talk about. This was the only thing, when I was around the courthouse, that people were interested in. When I went to the supermarket, people would stop me."

Again Ford leans back in his chair, and the questions about rape and publicity set him to philosophizing about how our litigious society is victimizing men. "Any woman can make a charge," he worries. "While the defendant has to be convicted beyond a reasonable doubt, for some reason people feel if the charge is made that there's truth to it." He points to Clarence Thomas as an example of this injustice, as well as the Navy's Tailhook sex scandal and the plethora of high-dollar sexual harassment suits in the business world. American law, he says, "is moving toward a position that favors the female or the person making the charge." Then he allows, "I suppose a man could make the charge too."

Acquaintance rape is another concern for Ford, "where somebody decides afterward that they didn't want to do it. If they said no at the time, and the act stopped, there would have been none. But later on to say, 'Well, I felt pressured to do it.' I think it puts both sides in a very difficult position. Rape used to be a clear-cut thing when I was a prosecutor," he remembers. "Unless there was some force involved, there wasn't any. Now it becomes subjective rather than objective. It's what one person says later against what one person denies." The system is being abused, he says, using the William Kennedy Smith case as an example. "Somebody dislikes somebody, they can make a charge. Twenty years from now, even if they're acquitted, people are going to say, 'I remember him, he's the guy who was charged with rape.' It's sort of off balance."

Ford is searching for another example, and he stumbles on the same one used by Carol Vasile when she was trying to illustrate the same point from her perspective. "Let me put it this way," he offers. "Robbery is robbery. In other words, if I have a gun and I take somebody's money, there's no question that's a crime. But if somebody has a sexual contact, they may not intend it to be a criminal act. It may have been something that the individual unwittingly or through saying nothing in a negative fashion encouraged. There still are going to be relationships between men and women," Ford acknowledges. "The question is, how do we differentiate between a criminal act and an act that is an act of affection, an act of love?" Ford is speaking faster now, warming to his subject; he seems to feel he has a handle on this crisis. "In other words, if you're going to take somebody's money with a gun, it's always a robbery, I don't give a damn whether it's your brother, your mother, or your wife. If you have a sexual act, in some instances it's going to be a loving, caring thing and in some instances it's going to be a crime—the same act." He stops and takes a breath. "That's the problem we face, evaluating and determining that."

■

Thomas Ford is not alone in his beliefs. Social critic and University of the Arts in Philadelphia humanities professor Camille Paglia joins him. In a 1991 article for New York *Newsday*, reprinted in her collection of essays, *Sex, Art, and American Culture*, she writes, "For a decade, feminists have drilled their disciples to say, 'Rape is a crime of violence but not of sex.' This sugar-coated Shirley Temple nonsense has exposed young women to disaster. Misled by feminism, they do not expect rape from nice boys from good homes who sit next to them in class."

While condemning rape, Paglia insists women must accept the risks involved in interacting with men. "The minute you go out with a man," she instructs in another of the essays, this one based on an interview with the *San Francisco Examiner*, "the minute you go to a bar to have a drink, there is risk. You have to accept the fact that part of the sizzle of sex comes from the danger of sex. You can be overpowered." Paglia too uses the William Kennedy Smith case to illustrate her point. "The girl in the Kennedy rape case is an idiot. You go back to the Kennedy compound late at night and you're surprised at what happens? She's the one who should be charged— with ignorance."

Included in the collected essays are Paglia's answers to questions about date rape posed to her by *YM* magazine. "Is it rape if she's too drunk to object?" Paglia is asked. "If she's drunk, she's complicitous," she believes, explaining her theory with this comparison: "If someone gets behind the wheel of a car drunk and mows down three people, you wouldn't excuse him because he started whining that he didn't mean it."

Another critic of women's movement assaults on acquaintance rape is former National Organization for Women board member Warren Farrell. In his book *The Myth of Male Power*, he declares, "Anyone who works with both sexes knows it is possible for a man to feel he's just made love and for a woman to feel she's been raped. It's also possible," concludes Farrell, "for a woman to feel she's made love in the evening when she's high, and feel raped in the morning when she's sober—without the man being a rapist. Or for a woman to feel she's been made love to one evening if the man said, 'I love you,' but feel raped the next morning if he hasn't called back."

Katie Roiphe joined the fray with her book, *The Morning After: Sex, Fear, and Feminism on Campus*. Based on her experiences as a student at Harvard and Princeton, Roiphe—whose mother, Annie Roiphe, wrote the feminist novel *Up the Sandbox*—charges her classmates with being too quick to identify themselves as victims, too quick to identify social mistakes as acquaintance rape. "If a woman's judgment is impaired, as they say, and she has sex," she writes about an intoxicated woman complaining the next day about rape, "it isn't always the man's fault; it isn't necessarily rape."

In her book, Roiphe attacks her mother's generation of feminists for misinterpreting just what constitutes acquaintance rape. "The idea that women can't withstand verbal or emotional pressure infantilizes them," she writes. One of her conclusions: "Everyone agrees that rape is a terrible thing, but we don't agree on what rape is. There is a gray area in which someone's rape may be another person's bad night."

These battle-of-the-sexes questions surround the debate about the Glen Ridge case despite the fact that Betty Harris's retardation adds a unique variable to the typical date rape, acquaintance rape, or even gang rape formula.

"I don't think we're victimizing men," says Robert Laurino when we discuss the debates within the feminist movement about rape. "I think most of the cases are very substantial," he says. The real problem is the opposite in Laurino's opinion: too many rape cases are not prosecuted because they are extraordinarily difficult to prove. Laurino wants to dispel the idea that if a woman runs into a prosecutor's office and cries out, "He raped me!" the man is automatically found guilty and sent to prison. "Back in Ford's day," he says about his opponent's history as a prosecutor, "there was almost a zero conviction rate. One of the reasons the unit I'm now heading up was started was that there was almost a zero conviction rate in this particular county. It's never going to be an equal playing field. Victims in sex crimes cases are always going to have an extra hurdle to overcome, at least in the immediate future. A lot of times it's only two people, the victim and the defendant. These are not the kinds of things that are committed out in public. So whenever you have this he said–she said type of situation, they are not easy—by any stretch of the imagination—to prove."

This is ground Laurino has thought through. He wants there to be no doubt about his position. "I don't really think that there is any victimization of men by any means," he says again. "There's been an extraordinary victimization of women."

■

As we continue to talk about these broader issues in his office, Thomas Ford lights into Carol Vasile and her partner from NOW. "Obviously those people had an ax to grind, a cause to press, " he says about their attendance at the trial. "They're the people who believe Anita Hill and disbelieve Clarence Thomas." I ask him what he perceives Vasile's ulterior motive to be, and he opens up with a litany of complaints. "Feminism as distinguished from mutuality. That women should be treated as a category, as a group. That it's not the human race, but that each group has its own segments." He makes a jump: "Obviously there are people that hate men, and these people may fit into that category. But we're talking philosophy now," he cautions, before returning to the specifics of the Glen Ridge case, repeating that he considers what his client did was morally wrong, but not illegal.

"I don't think any of them intended any hurt. She didn't intend to be hurt, they didn't intend to hurt her. What occurred is something that they mutually agreed on. I can think of other acts that would even be worse."

■

When they hear Ford's remarks repeated, the prosecutors' laughs are derisive. "When you look at the size of those implements," Laurino says about the broom and bat used against Betty, "particularly that bat, when you hear her describe what they were trying to do, when you hear the testimony as far as the boys trying to force it in, that it wasn't going in, it is just kind of beyond comprehension that somebody would make a request for an object of that nature to be inserted. It seemed like the boys at that point were getting downright frustrated. They kept pushing and pushing, and it wasn't going in. They kind of gave up out of almost disgust."

"Almost like using her as this lab rat," interjects Miller-Hall, "that they were going to do a science experiment on. What's the biggest object that you can insert into this science experiment? I think all you're hearing is the desire on Tom Ford and Michael Querques's part to believe it. They want to believe it. They want to believe that somehow the victim wanted this, that somehow it's just some strange aberration on sex and that she's not retarded and that she had the ability to at least attempt to stop this. They just want to believe that," she says again.

■

Ford gets up and struts back and forth around his office in much the same pompous manner he uses in the courtroom. I ask him if he second-guesses his decision to keep Christopher Archer off the witness stand. "I really don't think it affected the case," he responds. "They wouldn't have denied what happened," he says about all four of the rapists. "They would have said, 'Yes, we did the broom. Yes, we did the bat. But this is why.'" Perhaps, he muses as we say good-bye, such testimony would have convinced the jury.

■

Not a chance, prosecutor Glenn Goldberg tells me later. He is disappointed not to get a chance to grill the four defendants during the trial. Goldberg wants to ask them precisely the question Ford said they would have tried to answer: why they, as Ford put it, "did the bat" and "did the broom."

"I think the reason they didn't testify," says Goldberg, "is because they weren't prepared to answer those questions or to explain themselves to the jury."

Sex
and the
Retarded

16

I t was always our position from the beginning," Robert Laurino
insists, "that we have no problem in regards to the retarded
being able to engage in a normal, healthy sexual relationship.
But this was just pure, unmitigated violence. When you're
using implements of this nature, and there's no real gratification for
the boys, this was just pure violence and degradation." New Jersey
law specifically differentiates between those mentally retarded people who are capable of making their own decisions about sexual
activity and those defined as mentally defective, who do not ade-
quately understand what sex is all about and do not grasp their right
to refuse sex.

For much of this century, institutionalized retarded women were
subject to forced sterilization—a procedure the U.S. Supreme Court
ruled constitutional in a Virginia test case in 1927. The operation
was officially performed in Virginia through 1974. Before the practice stopped, at least 50,000 retarded Americans throughout the
country were sterilized in this example of eugenics and prejudice
against the mentally disabled. Today, the right to engage in sex with
a retarded person—and consequently retarded people's rights to a
sex life—is determined case by case. In New Jersey, for example,
N.J.S.A. 2C:14-2 specifically prohibits sex—even consensual sex—
with a mentally defective person who "is unable to comprehend the

distinctively sexual nature of the conduct or is incapable of understanding or exercising the right to refuse to engage in such conduct
with another."

As the Glen Ridge case unfolded, advocates for the rights of
retarded people were concerned that their successful efforts to dispel long-held societal prejudices against the mentally handicapped
would suffer reverses. With the defense calling Betty sex-crazed and
the prosecution calling her incompetent to make her own decisions
in regard to sex, their fears increased that stereotypes about the
retarded were being reinforced.

■

Betty Harris's plaintive call for help when she first reported the
attack against her was, "How do I say no?" That simple question
haunts the Glen Ridge rape case, a reminder of just how susceptible
Betty was, what perfect prey she was for the abuse the four rapists
planned for her.

"If she had been in my school," Leslie Walker-Hirsch tells me, she
may well have learned how to say no. She would have been taught
how to determine "who are the people you want to have that close—
in an intimate situation—and what are the qualities and character-
istics that you want them to have." Walker-Hirsch is president of the
Special Interest Group on Social and Sexual Concerns for the
American Association on Mental Retardation, an organization of
mental health care professionals involved in public policy development, research, and education. A psychologist, she specializes in
sexuality issues for people with mental retardation. She is the
author of a teaching curriculum designed to help the retarded
understand the social issues involved in human sexuality. Her work
includes teaching retarded people how to make day-to-day decisions
about sex, and she lobbies schools, trying to convince them of the
pressing need to develop special sex education classes for the
mentally retarded.

"The question isn't really about saying no," Walker-Hirsch says
about Betty's desperation. "The question is about how do I assert

myself without hurting the other person? How do I create clear boundaries for where my limits are?" The Walker-Hirsch technique offers the retarded three specific steps to follow if another person tries to overstep those boundaries. The first is to say, "Stop." The next is to physically leave the location where the offensive interaction is taking place as soon as possible. The third is to tell a so-called safe person what happened. It's a "boilerplate" system that can be used by anyone, she says.

Nonetheless, handicapped people often don't know where the boundary is, and so, she says, "they don't recognize when someone is overstepping it and consequently don't recognize the abuse until after the fact. They feel awful after."

Society has long been prejudiced against the idea of the mentally retarded as sexually active. Concerns about pregnancy fueled some of the repression experienced in the relatively recent past by the mentally handicapped. Not only were legitimate questions raised about child care for offspring of retarded couples, but it was commonly and erroneously believed that retardation was an inherited defect. At the same time, stereotypes developed casting the mentally retarded as exceptionally promiscuous.

"A person who is devalued because of her disability"—Walker-Hirsch is speaking generally, but her description fits Betty perfectly —"and has a low sense of worth is often likely to be very compliant and do pretty much anything to be liked. We have socialized her to be cooperative, to be docile, to do what she's told, to do what the authorities who know better and know more and are smarter say to do." Walker-Hirsch criticizes the tendency in the United States to deal with disabilities superficially and to integrate the handicapped into mainstream society without adequate preparation. "Often the only value that you are admired for or used for," she says about women in general who have been devalued by others, "is as a sexual object." Such a fate is even more common for retarded women because "they don't have the intellectual support and emotional support that we all have when we do meet people who devalue us and want us to only be sexual objects."

Based on that analysis, it is easy from for Walker-Hirsch to understand Betty's passive response in the Scherzer basement. "A person with a low sense of themselves, who wants to be liked, who wants to be included, who probably had more than the usual number of assaults to their self-esteem, is a perfect target for an incident where someone will take advantage of them sexually."

Walker-Hirsch also finds it easy to understand why the gang of rapists chose Betty as their victim. Again, stereotypes come into play. "There are some who say people with mental retardation make very good victims because when they talk, nobody listens, nobody believes them. Because they sometimes have cognitive disabilities that relate to time and place, or their language skills are poor, or they're easily confused, they get nervous when they start to have difficulty with words, they don't make very credible witnesses on their own behalf. So a person with a disability might be viewed as somebody who would make a good victim because they wouldn't report it."

Betty's courage on the witness stand, the perseverance of the prosecutors, and the tough verdict from the jury may all help make the Glen Ridge case a turning point in terms of justice for mentally handicapped victims of rape. The proceedings, despite Judge Cohen's sentence, made it clear that such complex cases can be adjudicated successfully.

For Leslie Walker-Hirsch and her colleagues, the challenge is to provide the mentally handicapped with the tools to prevent crimes from being committed against them. "People with mental retardation who have not been given specialized education are more vulnerable." Unless social skills and sexual skills are specifically taught, there is no reason to believe that the retarded will learn them just because they are exposed to them. "People like you and me,"she tells me, "you watch your older brother, you see people in a movie, you absorb a lot of information about how people interrelate together that's never taught directly. It's almost as if it just seeps into your skin. You observe it very casually—we call it incidental learning—it's not really taught to you." Incidental learning is not effective for people with mental retardation.

Betty's lack of the kind of specialized education taught by Walker-Hirsch and her peers is no excuse for the crime that was committed against her. "These guys knew she was handicapped." Walker-Hirsch is convinced by the testimony. "They'd grown up in the same town with her. They knew she was disabled. Rather than treat her more kindly and with greater personal responsibility, they used that on her to place her in a situation that was clearly beyond her scope. The victim is not to blame. No matter what she did or didn't do, these guys knew that she was less able and less capable of sorting this out than they were. That's why they selected her. Whatever she did or didn't do, I don't think that's an issue." She dismisses the defense lawyers' arguments—especially Querques's Lolita defense. "The issue is about what they did."

As we talk, Walker-Hirsch becomes increasingly vociferous about the rapists, their backgrounds, their lack of responsibility. "I really do think that football players—violent sportsmen—are taught to disregard the feelings of their opponents and to objectify them and not to have any empathy for the pain they may be causing them or what it means to hurl yourself at another person and knock them down and push them to the ground and violently press your ball to the goal line. I can't help but feel that this is the way that these guys have gained self-esteem, by disregarding the feelings of others and that they've been taught to do that as members of the football team." This training, she believes, helped them rationalize the crimes they committed.

Just as their classmate Josh Golin made clear, Walker-Hirsch identifies a perverted double standard in the rapists' behavior. "I would be relatively certain that these guys, when they go out with their regular dates, that they never suggest a baseball bat. And if their dates would suggest a baseball bat they would think it was about the most bizarre thing they'd ever heard. I don't think they do this with their regular dates."

Current treatment trends for people with mental retardation result in less institutionalization and more attempts to integrate those with developmental disabilities (the jargon preferred by many psychologists) into mainstream society than in the past. "People with retardation are now living on their own much more successfully than they ever have been before," Walker-Hirsch reminds me when I ask her why she thinks the Glen Ridge case captured the attention of so many observers. This new independence and the freedoms that come with it are forcing further study of sex among the retarded. "I think the topic has become ripe as the developmentally disabled people in the community have become more normal and more accepted as part of the community," she says. "The inequities in this case really touched everyone. You have the courtroom filled with these hulking guys and this one poor woman, who is very confused and has difficulty sorting things out, up against these large, looming, well-heeled guys. It's like they've got all the cards, and she's got fewer cards than most people. It's compelling, the poignancy."

Walker-Hirsch, as well as many other advocates for the mentally retarded, is disturbed by the repeated references to Betty Harris as an adult with the mind of an eight-year-old. "I hate that," she tells me, her voice sad. "A person who is eight, is eight," she explains simply, "and a person who has an IQ of sixty-four is not the same as a girl of eight. It's very misleading," she says about the characterization of Betty's mental ability. "Socially, the person may be more or less sophisticated and able than they are in math," she offers as an example, "and that would not be reflected when you see an aggregate IQ score. A person does not have the same abilities across the board. There are a number of different domains that are measured when you come up with that aggregate, and they don't all come out on the same line, or even near the same line, many times."

Her upset is understandable. Betty Harris is not eight. At the time of the rape, she had lived seventeen years; she had accumulated seventeen years of varied life experiences. She had nine more years to learn about life than an eight-year-old, even if her intelligence can be measured, for the purpose of better understanding her limitations, at the level of an eight-year-old. And, of great magnitude to the Glen Ridge case, Betty Harris's body at seventeen was the body of a seventeen-year-old, not the body of an eight-year-old. Her emotions were not limited to those of an eight-year-old; they were affected by her normal hormonal development. Physical sensations for Betty, including sexual sensations, were not limited to those of an average eight -year-old. "She just is not eight," says Walker-Hirsch with frustration. "It's just not the same."

■

"This is a criminal trial," Judge Cohen had instructed the jury as it was about to start deliberations. "It is not a morality play." The jurors watched him intently as he spoke. "You are not asked to decide whether what any of the defendants may have done was right or wrong in a moral sense."

Alice Vachss heard the judge's message just as her book on rape, *Sex Crimes*, was being released. "The judge says this is not a morality play," she told reporters, "but for us it is. We have to see it as a message to the society. And the message may be that we as a society cannot protect our most vulnerable members."

Vachss's agenda includes preaching the message that society must be protected from sex offenders, a type of criminal she's convinced rarely responds to rehabilitation efforts. "Saying victims cause rape," she writes, "is like saying banks cause robberies. No one deserves to be raped."

The former chief of the Special Victims Bureau in the Queens District Attorney's office in New York City, Vachss dismisses the idea that rapists are sick. "When sex offenders are caught," she insists in *Sex Crimes*, "and if they perceive serious consequences, they demand 'treatment,' even though no one is claiming to have found a 'cure.' The only viable 'treatment' for rape is quarantine. There is a lot of talk about sex-offender therapy, but there is only one functional diagnostic criterion: dangerousness. We spend much too much time trying to 'understand' rapists from a treatment point of view. If rapists are to be studied, we should study them from a combat point of view; we need to understand the enemy. Most fundamentally, what we need to know about rapists is how to interdict them, and how to put them down for the count once they are finally captured."

17.

The Prosecutors' Final Reflections

T he weather is muggy and thick on a late summer morning as I wait at the door of the New Courts Building in Newark for the distracted guard to study the x-ray picture of my satchel. He and his buddies are busy debating where to go for their lunch. He backs up the conveyer belt and takes a second look at the guts of my tape recorder before passing me into the lobby. The scene is routine and quiet—no harried news conference presided over by Thomas Ford, no jam of photographers chasing the Glen Ridge rapists for another picture showing their jut-jawed arrogance. It has been several months since the four of them were sentenced, and the attention their trial brought to the Essex County Courthouse is long gone.

In a back room of the prosecutor's wing of the building, I push a doll out of the way on a low table and pull my notebook out of my bag. Assistant prosecutors Glenn Goldberg, Robert Laurino, and Elizabeth Miller-Hall join me in a room the prosecutors usually use to interview children who are crime victims. It is crowded with a blackboard, dolls and stuffed animals, books for children, and little chairs. And it is hot.

Graying at the temples, his tie loosened and his shirt short-sleeves rolled up in the stuffy weather, Laurino does much of the talking. Intense and articulate, he is anxious to express his opinion—the opinion of a man who sees the seamy side of Essex County daily as he goes after the lawbreakers. "I see implements," says Laurino about the other cases he works on. "It's not really very unusual." He specializes in sex crimes and says foreign object rape certainly is not, as he puts it, "your average case," but in the sordid world of violent rape, he experiences the worst.

"I've had cases where things like flashlights, tree limbs...." He thinks through the cases he's tried and studied. "I've seen things like Coke bottles, different types of objects being used in vaginal cavities. In and of itself," he says about foreign object rape, "that isn't that unusual." Among his rape cases, he estimates "one out of ten might have some type of implement other than normal penile-vaginal sex. It could be a hand or finger. That is not uncommon." But in combination with other captivating aspects of the crime— such as Betty's mental impairment and the relative affluence of the rapists—the public and the press became fascinated by the use of foreign objects in this rape case. In addition to the elements inherent in the crime that make it intriguing, the Glen Ridge rape provided a social counterpoint to the Central Park jogger case, involving a brutal attack by a poorer, urban gang on a young and successful New York career woman.

"People have so many misconceptions about rape," Elizabeth Miller-Hall says, suggesting that the Glen Ridge case "brought to life this idea that you're dealing with something that can be very violent and that a sense of degradation can be involved—and it's not sexual." Miller-Hall is intense, too, as she speaks, gesturing with her hands. A gold bracelet flashes on her wrist. Periodically she pulls on the hem of her long dress as it rides up her leg, exposing her slip. "They picked a victim," she says about the Glen Ridge gang, "who is very vulnerable but is not viewed as a classic sort of rape victim—as being a sexual thing."

Is rape sex or is it violence, especially a rape such as the one perpetrated in the Scherzers' basement, where it seems there was little or no physical sexual gratification for the criminals? Laurino doesn't hesitate: "It's really a combination of both," he says.

The three prosecutors are pleased with themselves, and they

show it. They tried a difficult and controversial case, and they won guilty verdicts from the jury. As we discuss the strategies they used and the criticisms directed toward them by the defense lawyers, they put an end to debate about their techniques with the observation that the State of New Jersey won the case.

But what about the relatively light sentences? As we sit talking in the hot, humid children's interview room, Christopher Archer, the Scherzer twins, and Bryant Grober are recovering from a night of barhopping or taking in the sun at the Jersey Shore or preparing for the start of a new school semester or working at a summer job. For these convicted and sentenced rapists, life continues relatively normally.

Laurino expresses his disappointment, but despite complaints about the sentencing, he is pleased with the results of their work. "I think you have to look at the larger picture. We weren't successful with our arguments for sentencing. But overall, the case really broke ground." The fact that the prosecutor's office decided to press charges at all is something he is proud to be part of. "In rape cases in general"—Laurino wants to make sure this point is understood—"juries want pristine victims—vestal virgins. They don't want a victim that is in any manner impaired. Once you have a victim in any rape case that has any type of past sexual history, and you throw in the problems of this mental impairment, it's extraordinarily difficult. Juries don't like these types of cases." Laurino and his colleagues feel they made it easier for other prosecutors to try similarly complex rape cases in the future because they went ahead with the Glen Ridge case, even though Betty's past promiscuity and mental retardation had the potential to weaken her credibility as a witness. Laurino lists the other results of the case that make him proud: "We made law in New Jersey regarding coercion. We now have rape trauma syndrome recognized in this state. It was disappointing in the end," he says again, "but there was a larger victory overall."

I remind the three prosecutors that, for all their successes, the guilty are running around Essex County while we talk about their crimes. "Yup," says Laurino, with his experienced voice of acceptance, "they're out. Uh-huh."

"That just must be disconcerting," I say. "It must be annoying to you."

Elizabeth Miller-Hall readily agrees, but is thinking about frustration beyond her office. "I think it's probably more disconcerting for rape victims or other women out there who look at this. Here you've got a case where the system did work. You have a prosecutor's office that's not only saying that rape is a serious crime, we're also saying that rape upon someone who is the most vulnerable and almost a forgotten type of person in our society is a serious crime. Then you have a jury that understands this. And this makes other victims feel that maybe society itself is changing." She is pounding one hand against the other as she makes her points, her eyes wide; she is emotional in her support for using the law to remedy wrongs. "Obviously, it would have been nicer from our perspective if they would have been remanded immediately or the actual sentence was a little bit more," but she too voices a professional acceptance of the reality of the soft treatment. She and the others are investigating and trying other cases now, attempting to send other criminals to Rahway State Prison.

"We're very upset," says Laurino, "but we did everything we possibly could."

Of the three of them, Glenn Goldberg is the quietest. He sits and watches and listens as we talk, only periodically offering his often caustic remarks. Goldberg is the prosecutor who sang the Simon and Garfunkel tune "The Sounds of Silence" as he was summing up the prosecution's case during the trial. Although he denied behaving inappropriately, he was drawing the jury's attention to the fact that the four defendants did not testify. Defense lawyers say his singing is one of their grounds for an appeal, since the defendants were well within their Fifth Amendment rights to remain silent.

"On a more positive point," Goldberg finally interjects, "while we would have wanted them to be incarcerated immediately—as we felt they should be, and most people felt—and it would have been more satisfying had that occurred, the fact of the matter is that they're probably punished more to the extent that the sentences hang over their heads. Ultimately," he says with conviction, "when their appeals are rejected, they will go to jail."

Maybe. Maybe not. The rapists' old classmates see them around Glen Ridge, Bloomfield, and the Oranges, hanging out in the bars, enjoying the nightclub scene. Once again the Big Men on Campus beat the system—at least for now. The cocky arrogance of their appearances in court continues in their community.

Investigators from the prosecutor's office follow them. "We don't have anybody out there looking after their every move," says Laurino, but his office tries to keep track of them through informants and the local police forces. "Apparently they're back to life as normal, back to the bar scene, back to the Shore," says Goldberg. "So, to that extent, I don't think they really felt the impact of the sentence. Judgment day has been postponed so long for them. This is now going on five years since the act, and nothing has been done. They talk about swift punishment being a deterrent and being probably the most effective means of punishment, and that's been totally absent in this case."

A summer at the Shore and in the bars bothers Miller-Hall, too. "From my perspective," she says, exasperated, "they just didn't get it. They don't see the harm that was created." She describes their attitudes as "cavalier" and cannot understand their lack of remorse and their inability to question their actions or doubt the validity of their behavior.

Equally difficult to understand is the motive for the crime. "When you look at the history with these boys, Betty was always subject to their taunting, their ridicule," Laurino reminds me. He repeats that his experience proves that as abhorrent as the Glen Ridge case may be to most observers, its criminal elements are relatively common. The case, he worries, "may be a reflection of how society views their more vulnerable people, people who may not be considered a whole person. These boys, particularly the Archer boys, had teased her. They called her 'stupid,' they called her 'retard,' and a few other things along those lines. She was pretty much the object of their derision over the years. Betty almost became the town fool."

The job of the State in a criminal trial is not to prove why a criminal commits a crime. What must be proved beyond a reasonable doubt is only that the defendant is the guilty party. Yet I keep asking these successful prosecutors to try to explain why the four rapists would do such a thing. After immersing themselves in the crime and the lives of the victim, the perpetrators, and all the other characters in the drama, these prosecutors are in an ideal position to speculate about motive. Did the society that produced them—their close-knit and affluent suburb—fail? Are their parents to blame? Their school and teachers?

Miller-Hall breaks into my question as I again reflect on their status at school: athletic heroes admired by their peers. "It meant that they were in a town that rewarded athletes and attractive boys but that didn't mean that they received any sort of sense of morality." She brings up the theory that the skewed priorities of Glen Ridge society adversely affected their development. "To some degree, maybe that encouragement they received that they are so above everyone made them feel that they can do whatever they feel to anyone."

I can easily understand the elevated relationship the four rapists enjoyed with the rest of the town, I tell the prosecutors. What I seek help understanding is what motivated these boys to make the jump from heroes to criminals. Elizabeth Miller-Hall looks at me, and I judge from her reflective expression that she is flipping through her mental file of equally repugnant crimes and criminals. "You look at history," she reminds me, "and people do an awful number of cruel things to other people on a vast scale. It just seems to be part of the down side of human nature."

"We're not sociologists," Glenn Goldberg says, steering our conversation away from a visceral and emotional response to all the bad guys in the world, "and, of course, it's not our job necessarily to figure out why criminals do what they do. In very simple terms, I think common sense indicates that in this case there was some element of showing off. These guys were showing off to one another. Betty was almost the ideal victim—an object that they could use to show off to each other, exercise their control and power over, and enhance, they felt, their own self-esteem in the eyes of their fellow sports figures."

I ask the three of them to speculate about how showing off progresses into abusive, criminal behavior. Again Miller-Hall contends that some criminal behavior is beyond comprehension for most people. "Hopefully," she says, "you can never fully understand it. I think if you can fully understand it, you've almost passed that line," she laughs, referring to the barrier that separates the good guys from the bad guys. "You don't want to fully be able to get into their heads and understand why they could do something like this to someone else."

■

Betty Harris, as the prosecutors make clear to me, was not an ideal rape victim from their professional standpoint. Her active sex life, the questions of credibility that developed from her mental retardation, and her willing participation in the Scherzer basement activities all conspired to create a formidable challenge for the State.

"We wanted to present the case in a way that would get people to understand this girl, Betty." Laurino is explaining the prosecution's basic strategy. "People should know who she is and get to know her through people who knew her—friends, people in education, and even strangers who saw her interaction with others and saw how these boys treated her." Using testimony from both experts and people who routinely encountered Betty, the prosecutors hoped to prepare the jury for Betty's testimony. After her court appearance, says Laurino, the prosecutors worked to present witnesses who could explain to the jury what Betty's testimony meant to the case. "I think it was an extraordinarily successful strategy," he concludes contentedly, and his colleagues join him in self-congratulatory post-trial summation.

■

The three are just as quick to ridicule the failed "boys-will-be-boys" defense attempted by Michael Querques. They even pronounce his name with amusement: quirk-ease. "I guess he's an older man, and he's a product of his times," considers Laurino. Miller-Hall is much more direct with her criticism. "It was quite clear that he saw women as being only objects and not human beings," she says with staccato deliberateness. She remembers her reaction as the defense stumbled along: "It was extraordinary that he didn't even realize what he was saying."

Even if a jury could accept the concept of "boys will be boys," with its broader sense of youthful experimentation, it was a failed defense, says Laurino, because of the foreign object attack perpetrated by the rapists. "They went that extra step beyond being foolarounds," he says. "Once you begin getting those objects—that, in particular, made an impression on this jury."

Miller-Hall returns to Querques's characterization of women in general. "It was so much his view that women aren't human." She interprets Querques's bizarre remarks comparing his daughters' physical attributes for the jury. "His message was that to some degree a victim is to blame for what happens to her," Miller-Hall says, and that "these boys, or men, in our society have the right to do what they feel like doing. He seemed to buy this idea that they had the right to do whatever they felt like doing to this victim."

"He also turned it," remembered Laurino, "and tried to make Betty this siren, the Lolita opening that he did."

"But a siren based on how she physically looked," Miller-Hall interjects with irritation. "Her body structure made her into something that caused them to do what they had to do."

"And so these boys were ensnared." Laurino finishes his interpretation of the Querques argument with disgust.

"All of us women should go and have plastic surgery," mocks Miller-Hall, "to prevent boys from being boys and raping."

"I think in this case he hit on some of the themes that people were thinking of," says Laurino, acknowledging that Querques's thesis could have worked and that it was his presentation that failed. "But what he did was to be just so overt that it backfired."

The jury's verdict clearly shows that Querques's tactics were a failure, points out Goldberg. They "would not work, could not work, and did not work," he says with finality. "The general outcry from the community," he says, proves that Querques's interpretation of just what constitutes rape and his attitudes about women are "not in keeping with present-day thought or present-day philosophy. If anything, it further gave rise to putting those beliefs to rest and demonstrated for future reference of trial attorneys that that type of philosophy and tactic will not work for them."

■

Our conversation turns to the pivotal point of the crime, to the pivotal point of the trial. Betty did descend willingly into the Scherzer basement; she complied with the gang's demands; she was ambivalent on the witness stand about being harmed. What, I ask, persuaded the jury to interpret the events of that afternoon as criminal? Why didn't they view Betty as culpable?

The answer comes from Laurino. "I think her impairment was the overriding factor, that it wasn't so much that she was culpable, but that she was being used. I think in most rape cases, juries look at the victim and believe that there's a degree of personal responsibility that the person should have and, once that victim maybe crosses the line, then there is a consideration on the jury's part that the victim may have encouraged or helped to promote the incident.

"In Betty's case, Betty was so impaired, and these boys knew it. They knew what buttons to push to get her to the basement, to say that Paul Archer, the person that she adored, would be there and she would get a date from him. Betty is gullible enough to fall for that. The average girl would not be. But in the case of Betty, that was the perfect line and they knew how to get Betty there."

Not an
Isolated
Case

18

W hile the Glen Ridge rapists were on trial, another disconcertingly similar scandal surfaced on the West
Coast. Nine Lakewood High School boys in suburban
Los Angeles were charged with molesting and raping
neighbor girls as young as ten years old. They were members of a
club called Spur Posse, a subculture loosely organized by a couple
of dozen bored Lakewood buddies looking to link themselves to
each other by the quantity of their sexual encounters.

Spur Posse was set up as a competition—at the time of the arrests,
nineteen-year-old Billy Shehan was winning. Billy boasted sixty-six
notches in his belt. Harder to understand is the pride some of the
Posse parents expressed to reporter Jane Gross of the *New York Times*
when she canvassed Lakewood studying the story. "Aren't they virile
specimens?" Tom Belman asked Gross rhetorically about his two
sons, one the brains behind the Posse, the other fresh out of jail and
still facing rape charges. Other astounding one-liners came from the
elder Belman. He explained that the girls in question were "giving
it away," and he insisted that "there wouldn't be enough jails in
America" to lock up boys for doing what his do. Billy Shehan's father
blamed society with this rationalization: "I don't see these kids acting
much different from professional athletes, like when Wilt Chamber-
lain came out with his book and said he had 20,000 women."

There is no suggestion that the victims of Spur Posse were mentally retarded, but it is a felony in California to engage in sexual intercourse with a minor, and ten years is just slightly older than the mental age attributed to the Glen Ridge victim.

Charges eventually were dropped against eight of the nine—the district attorney decided convincing a jury that the girls did not consent would be virtually impossible because the girls involved probably consented to some sex with some Spur Posse members. The boy charged with molesting the ten-year-old did not contest the charges; he was sentenced to a juvenile facility for less than a year. "These were fourteen- and fifteen-year-old girls, who were unsure of themselves and wanted to be liked," L.A. sheriff's commander Robert Ripley told Amy Cunningham for her *Glamour* magazine article. "You reach a point where you have to wonder what's coercion."

Echoing Michael Querques's Glen Ridge opening argument, the mother of one of the Spur Posse gang told *Time* magazine, "What can you do? It's a testosterone thing." As in Glen Ridge, the student body at Lakewood High become split—some were disgusted, others wore black armbands to show support for their arrested classmates.

About the same time, as I stopped at a market along the Chesapeake Bay, a headline in the Annapolis *Capital* caught my eye: BROTHERS FACE RAPE CHARGES. The sub-headline especially grabbed my attention because of my immersion in the Glen Ridge case: GIRL: IT HAPPENED AT HIGH SCHOOL PARTY.

The story is depressingly familiar. A party along the West River. Drinking. A sixteen-year-old girl passed out in the driveway. The sixteen- and seventeen-year-old brothers, friends of the girl told police, lifted her up, laid her out in the back of a pickup truck, and took turns violating her. The friends say they witnessed the attack and tried to stop the rape but were afraid of the brothers, who threatened them later if they called the police. The father expressed shock when the boys were charged as adults for a crime that carries a maximum penalty in Maryland of life in prison. "They have girls coming to the house all the time," he said. "From what I understand, this is a mutual thing."

Although there was no suggestion that the West River girl was retarded, passed-out drunk certainly means that she too was in no position to say no.

Just a few days later, in Baltimore County, Maryland Circuit Court Judge Thomas Bollinger drew criticism from local politicians, negative press coverage, and public outrage after sentencing a rapist to a brief period of probation. The victim was a teenager, the middle-aged rapist once her boss. The penalty could have been twenty years in prison. Again, the victim's ability to say no was a crucial element of the case.

But it was not only the harmless penalty that riled Marylanders when they first read of Judge Bollinger's decision in the *Baltimore Sun*. His good-old-boy analysis of the crime, the criminal, and the victim proved yet again that rape victims often suffer a judicial violation if they press charges against their attackers.

Drink was once more part of the problem in this story. An underage girl spent an evening with several friends drinking hard at a Towson, Maryland, bar. Too drunk to care for herself, the girl was helped by her buddies to the adjacent apartment of Lawrence Gillette, at one time the manager of a local movie house. Once at his apartment, the girl threw up and passed out in Gillette's bed.

When she next regained consciousness, she testified, Lawrence Gillette was "on top of me." She recognized him, she told the court, and passed out again. Gillette did not dispute engaging in sexual intercourse with the girl but claimed that it was a consensual act and one during which the girl was fully conscious. Consciousness is a key element here because by the definition of second-degree rape in Maryland, intercourse with an unconscious woman is illegal. The crucial wording in the law is "mentally incapacitated" and "physically helpless." The law specifically includes intoxication when it defines what constitutes an incapacitated and helpless state of mind and body. And the verdict in the Towson case was rape; Gillette was found guilty of raping his unconscious victim.

From the bench, Judge Bollinger flabbergasted his critics by accusing the victim as he passed his light sentence on her attacker, saying she "was contributorily negligent by putting herself in this situation." The judge then ridiculed the Maryland law he was obligated to enforce, saying the "victim facilitated the crime."

Again, this is a case in which the woman was mentally incapacitated and unable to make a decision. The judge responded with a boys-will-be-boys attitude, even though this boy was forty-four years old. "The dream of quite a lot of males, quite honestly," Judge Bollinger called intercourse with an unconscious partner.

"I'm stunned," was the response of one state legislator, Senator Mary Boergers. "This is like a throwback to thirty or forty years ago," she complained, calling for disciplinary action against the judge. "It's outrageous to think that it's all right to have intercourse with someone when they're not aware of it." Her colleague, Senator Janice Piccinini, called the judge's words and actions "incomprehensible in this day and age," especially since "Maryland has been on the leading edge of recognizing rape as an act of violence and that women aren't chattel."

A handful of demented dentists are identified as rapists in New York prosecutor Linda Fairstein's book *Sexual Violence*—rapists who take advantage of women they incapacitate with anesthesia while fixing their teeth. Fairstein acknowledges her difficulty in understanding the motivation behind their crimes. "An individual like Teicher," she writes about fifty-three-year-old Marvin Teicher, whom she sent to jail after proving he molested two patients and a police decoy, "and the many like him, is really a conundrum to most of us. He is an educated man with a professional degree. He had practiced dentistry for more than two decades. He had a fine family, a fancy suburban house, and many friends in the community."

One dentist apologized after Fairstein orchestrated a telephone conversation between him and his victim. The victim, using a script written by Fairstein, elicited a confession from him, and he then promised to fix his victim's teeth free—as compensation. "Our success in getting admissions from sex offenders on tape never ceases to amaze me," writes Fairstein.

She finds that although street-wise rapists rarely confess to their victims, upper-middle-class men often do. "For these offenders," she concludes, "the words 'involuntary' and 'without consent' seem to have no meaning at all." She makes a generalization about such types of criminals, a generalization that describes the Glen Ridge rapists: "These are people who put their own needs and desires ahead of the personal dignity of other human beings. These offenders *know* that what they are doing is wrong and not in conformity with the rules of society. The tragedy is that they just do not care."

Shortly after the Scherzers, Archer, and Grober were sentenced, police in Montclair, the next town up Bloomfield Avenue from Glen Ridge, stumbled on at least seven teenage boys who apparently were not deterred by the Glen Ridge rape case. The seven were identified by police as members of a gang calling themselves the Hardhedz Posse, a roving band of tough punks who previously specialized in stealing bicycles and selling them. Three of the seven Hardhedz later arrested, say police reports, surprised a seventh-grade girl who was "a perfect victim." She was walking home from school. The Hardhedz dragged her, of all places, into a back building on the campus of St. Cassian's Church and School. There she was forced to perform oral sex on the gang members and masturbate them.

A few weeks later, the same girl was approached by five Hardhedz, including two who participated in the first attack. She and two girl-friends escaped into a temporary safe haven—the Bellevue Branch Library. But the predators staked out the library, and when the victim finally decided, along with one of her friends, to try to flee home, a Hardhedz member pedaling a bicycle caught the running girl and forced her back to Mt. Hebron School. The attack that followed is recounted in sordid detail by Jonathan Welsh and Sanford Jacobs in their article on the case in the weekly *Montclair Times*.

> Three gang members took her to the bottom of an outside stairway leading to a lower level entrance. While some gang members stood watch at the top of the stairway, others forced her to perform oral sex on them, police said.
>
> The friend who had been with her, however, returned to the school grounds and confronted the lookouts, loudly demanding to know what they had done with her friend, police sources said.

The girl could see boys at the bottom of the stairwell, but the victim wasn't visible from there, police said. The friend's persistence and the presence of a custodian, who had come outside, apparently caused the lookouts to yell down the stairwell, and the victim was released.

She ran up the stairs crying, and her hair, which had been pulled back in a ponytail, was loose and tangled because the boys had grabbed it to force her to do what they wanted, police said.

But the Hardhedz apparently were not finished with their abused victim. A couple of weeks later, during the school day, she made the mistake of walking to the toilet. Grabbed in the hallway, she was forced under another stairwell, where five boys demanded sex. And Montclair police identified one of the Hardhedz they say molested the Mt. Hebron student as being a partner in a similar attack on a thirteen-year-old Glenfield School seventh-grade student.

The Montclair police chief, Thomas Russo, was ready with a response when asked what connection he saw between the events unfolding in his jurisdiction and the Glen Ridge rape. "There is no correlation," he insisted. The Board of Education president Carolyn Nunery told parents not to worry. "Our schools have been and will continue to be safe," she said and offered counseling to all parents and students involved in the case.

But it was from North Carolina that some of the most disconcerting news came for those troubled by the Glen Ridge rape. It was New Year's Eve, right in the middle of the Glen Ridge trial. Five teenagers were picked up by Iredell County authorities and charged with raping a mentally handicapped woman whom one of the five had dated. The woman—nineteen at the time—functioned mentally at the level of a child.

On New Year's Eve, she told investigators, she was taken to an apartment, raped, and then penetrated with a broomstick. The following day, she said, she was taken to a construction site and raped again. The second time, her attackers recorded their actions on a videotape that was eventually seized by police. "I thought I'd get to go home," she explained to the court why she had not resisted her attackers, "and it would be all over."

■

None of these cases would unduly surprise specialists who deal with acquaintance rape and gang acquaintance rape. Certainly Joseph Weinberg is not surprised by the litany of cases with similarities to the Glen Ridge rape. Weinberg's rape-prevention work is headquartered in his home in Madison, Wisconsin. From there he organizes the speeches, training sessions, and interactive workshops he offers schools, businesses, and prisons through the group Men Stopping Rape. He arrived at this work through no formal academic training, but after a career as a carpenter and a contractor—experience he calls "a degree in hyper-masculinity." His essay, written with Michael Biernbaum and suggesting techniques for verbally creating an erotic atmosphere, is collected in the Milkweed anthology *Transforming a Rape Culture.*

"Oh, no, no, no," he said when I asked him if he sees the Glen Ridge case as a unique aberration. "It's entertainment," he categorized the Scherzer basement rape—entertainment as defined by the boys and men he works with who interact with one another in the same fashion as the claque of Glen Ridge athletes led by the Scherzers and the Archers. "Every fraternity I've been in talks with one degree or another of openness about their Fuck a Fat Chick Contest or their Fuck an Ugly Chick Contest. I hear this all the time, I confront this all the time." Weinberg is not alone calling attention to such events. Social psychologist Chris O'Sullivan found them called "pig contests" and "hog contests." These fraternity experiences, theorizes Dr. O'Sullivan in an essay in *Transforming a Rape Culture,* result in "victimizing and objectifying women, as well as alienating men from their own sexuality."

Seemingly unattractive women are chosen as targets because of their vulnerability, Weinberg believes—because such victims lack credibility if they complain. "If she is agreed to be unattractive, people tend to believe her less," he says, because a common reaction is "Why would anyone assault her if she's ugly?" In addition, he says, rapists involved in such contests find a potential defense in the line, "She must be lying because she must be appreciative of the attention."

Keeping score in terms of quantity is another common denominator Weinberg continually observes among fraternity brothers. "The motivation is to win points and prove to other males that we are heterosexuals and therefore not a threat in that arena. I think that the work of males in our life," he says sadly, based on his observations of modern American society, "is to prove to other males that we are heterosexual—that we all wear baseball hats backwards."

From his perspective as a student of the gang rape culture that too often develops among athletes and fraternity brothers, Weinberg believes the same type of mentality was at work when the Glen Ridge rapists sought out Betty Harris as when fraternities engage in their various contests. "She was anxious to please and wanted friends. I think back to when I was six, seven, eight, there was a retarded girl in the neighborhood, and the older guys would say, 'Estelle, take off your dress.' Estelle would take off her dress."

Weinberg uses the Glen Ridge case as a prime example when he makes his rape-prevention presentations. For one thing, he contrasts it with the vicious attack on the Central Park jogger—drawing attention to what he, along with so many others, is convinced is the racist aspect of the case. "If you're young and black," he says, referring to the criminals involved in the Central Park case, "you hang. It's the end of Western civilization. It's wolf pack; it's wilding. Buy guns; lock up the house. It's the end of the world." But, he says, when four attractive white men do it, it's "boys will be boys." Weinberg concludes that racism is at work when rape cases are adjudicated, a conclusion he makes based on casual observation and a visceral response—he can cite no statistical documentation.

The usual rape victim in a fraternity house, Weinberg has learned, involves an extremely drunk woman. He tries to impress on his students that the law in many states does not distinguish between retarded and asleep, drunk, and passed out. "Those are all unable to give consent." But he also tries to impress upon his audiences that the use of the baseball bat and broomstick should not be considered a greater offense than any other kind of unwanted penetration—despite the gruesome images that such a practice triggers in most people's imaginations. "I don't make a real strong distinction between a penis and a different foreign object. If it's coerced, I would not make a distinction that would set this case drastically far from any other assault."

Shame and guilt bring men to his encounter groups and lectures, believes Weinberg. "I find them wildly responsive to the discussion." Although he is convinced that the Glen Ridge rapists need to be punished, he hopes they will seek treatment, too, "starting with empathy for themselves and seeing who they are. Confront that behavior," he suggests. "Where did they learn to be men? What were the lessons? Why were they so incredibly insecure about themselves that nobody would say 'There's a problem here' and 'We're going too far' and 'This is ugly' and 'I don't like this, I want out.' They need to look at that."

There is little difference between the environments created by fraternities and the settings where the Glen Ridge rapists lived out their fantasies. The town itself is much like a college campus, removed from the rest of Essex County by its affluence, by so many stately homes with their sweeping grounds, by its incestuous sense of community. The Scherzers and the Archers and their ilk ran the most popular social group in their school, and they used their parents' homes like private frat houses. The Scherzers' grandmother was upstairs during the rape, working in the kitchen like a fraternity's housekeeper. The lifestyle of the Glen Ridge rapists combined the macho evils of out-of-control sports teams with the perversions of institutionalized fraternity house rape scenarios.

Weinberg attempts to prevent rape, seeking what he perceives to be high-risk men for his audiences. But what of rapists like the Glen Ridge criminals? Should they just be locked up, or are they candidates for treatment? Can they realize that what they did to Betty Harris was wrong? Can they be taught not to rape again? Can they be treated in addition to being punished?

On the east side of Baltimore, on a campus surrounded by tough neighborhoods, sits the Johns Hopkins University School of Medicine. There Dr. Fred Berlin is associate professor in the Psychiatry and Behavioral Sciences Department. Berlin attempts to cure sex criminals at the National Institute for the Study, Prevention, and Treatment of Sexual Trauma, where he serves as director. "I'm not sure you can punish the attitudes away," he says about men involved in attacks like the one perpetrated against Betty Harris. Although he is in the business of treating sex criminals, he believes that the criminal justice systems, as well the doctors, must be involved in many cases, and that there are situations in which the guilty should be locked up in prison. And there are cases in which the criminals are simply the bad guys, not clinically ill. But even some of those types can benefit from professional intervention. "Whether we call these people sick, I certainly don't want to just excuse their misconduct by saying it's a product of an illness. I'm not suggesting that. People can not be ill and still need help in terms of seeing the world differently, having a different appreciation of their responsibilities in it, having a different sense of the impact of their actions on others. I'm not necessarily suggesting that these people are mentally ill in a traditional sense and that they shouldn't be held accountable for their actions. That doesn't mean that punishment alone is necessarily going to solve the problem completely." Professional treatment dealing with why the men committed the crimes, Dr. Berlin believes, can lead to successful rehabilitation.

Were he asked to treat sex offenders such as the Glen Ridge rapists, Dr. Berlin told me he would first study their personal moral and ethical values. He would investigate the peer pressures that were involved in the crime and determine if the men objectified the victim and allowed themselves to ignore the fact that she is a distinct person. "I suspect that people like this," he said of gang rapists, "tend not to see the woman involved as a real person, having real feelings. They tend not to assume personal responsibility, sometimes abdicating that to the group, rather than any one of them thinking that they themselves are responsible individuals."

Once those issues were addressed, Dr. Berlin told me, he could consider a regimen of treatment for rapists such as those from Glen

Ridge. "I'm assuming that these people don't have a sexual disorder," says Dr. Berlin, "that they don't seem driven or compelled to act in such a fashion. It seems to me that we're most likely dealing with people who have particular sets of values and attitudes. The treatment"—and he says he hesitates to use the word *treatment* because he is not convinced a diagnosis would cite the rapists as sick—"would be to try to address that fact, to see if these individuals can be made to understand the effects of their actions on others, to recognize the kind of trauma that they may have induced in their victims, to recognize that sexual intimacy needs to involve mutual respect and a sense of caring and concern for the other person. Discussing those kinds of values, trying to instill within them some sense of that, would be, it seems to me, the mainstay of treatment in a case such as this."

At Dr. Berlin's institute, such treatment probably would be conducted in a group setting. "If this was a group situation to start with, it was presumably some negative peer pressure influencing these folks to think about things and to act in an improper way. Sometimes the most effective way to try to counteract that is with positive peer pressure, by placing them in groups with people who perhaps have learned to think about things more responsibly. Rather than feeling that they are getting a lecture from an authority figure, they hear from their own peers, who have begun to change their ways."

No form of treatment was mandated, or even recommended, by the court for the Glen Ridge rapists. But Dr. Berlin is convinced they would benefit from professional help. "I would suggest that if it is simply peer pressure and people suffer consequences and are forced to think about their actions, I don't necessarily see anything that would put them at high risk of continuing. Hopefully they would have learned a painful lesson and their prognosis for the future, if indeed they've learned that lesson, may not be so bad."

■

So who is at fault? What is at fault? Irresponsible parents? A lax high school administration? Accessible pornography? A popular culture in late twentieth-century America that parades sexually suggestive material on billboards, in the movies, through hit music, on TV, over the radio?

Late in July 1993, Larry King and his radio talk show audience were discussing the relationship between fictional violence depicted by the media and escalating levels of violence in American society. Dick Cavett called the show and reminded King about the popularity of comedy shows on TV. "How come if violence on television causes violence on the streets," wondered Cavett, "comedy on television doesn't cause comedy on the streets?"

Pornography, of course, predates the dirty videos that amused the Glen Ridge rapists throughout their high school years. "Hieroglyphics and cave drawings," speculated prosecutor Glenn Goldberg about sources for the earliest examples. But neither he nor his colleagues blame pornography for the crime committed in the Scherzer basement. "Those other major circumstances and forces" attract his attention: "sex, human nature, differences in people, inherent goodness, inherent badness—that's been around for thousands of years."

New York Daily News columnist Amy Pagnozzi quoted an explanation for the crime offered informally by defense lawyer Louis Esposito when he was chatting up one of Pagnozzi's male colleagues in one of the Essex County Courthouse corridors. "When you're eighteen years old," opined the lawyer, "your dick's on fire."

At the age of eighteen and throughout life, many men are filled —perhaps obsessed—with sexual desire. Most men do not rape. Few men gather their friends to probe the village idiot with bats and brooms. To understand the Glen Ridge story is to realize that it is not about Betty Harris's mental abilities or sexual experiences. It is certainly about consent. But mostly it is about four misguided criminals who clearly acted with evil intent.

Consent is being redefined by Americans. University of Southern California Law School professor Susan Estrich, a rape victim and author of *Real Rape*, says her research reveals that just a century ago there were judges deciding rape cases who believed that sexual intercourse was impossible if the woman did not consent to the act.

These days, an Indiana jury believed Mike Tyson's date when she testified at his rape trial that she joined him in the middle of the night at his hotel room but never intended to engage in sex with him. Just the two of them were in the room. There were no witnesses. He testified that she consented; she said he overpowered her and forced himself on her. The heavyweight champion went to prison. Yet the popularity of T-shirts screaming the slogan FREE MIKE TYSON indicates that the guilty verdict is not universally appreciated. The latent questions suggested by the FREE MIKE TYSON T-shirts are What was she doing in his room in the middle of the night if she didn't expect sex? Wasn't going to his room on a date at that hour a de facto consent to sex? What responsibilities must women assume for their own protection from unwanted sex?

The issues were similar at the William Kennedy Smith trial, and there the jury quickly decided that the woman Smith picked up in a bar and took home for more partying was not a victim of rape. Her party-girl history may or may not have tainted the jury; it surely influenced the public opinion that developed against her.

Consent was the issue in Austin, Texas, when Joel Rene Valdez broke into a woman's apartment, threatened her with a knife, and demanded sex. "She asked me to do her a favor, and I did," Valdez testified. "She told me to put on a condom, and I did." The defense claimed her request that he protect her from disease and impregnation implied consent to sex. Initially, a Texas grand jury agreed with Valdez's argument and refused to indict him. After a second grand jury handed down an indictment, he was tried, convicted, and sentenced to forty years in state prison.

"I am Xan Wilson," the woman who brought the charges against Valdez told the jury after they announced the sentence. "In the past, I've been known as the condom rape victim. I am not the condom rape victim. I do not have the victim's mentality. I am a survivor of rape, which is a violent crime." Wilson, calling her experience a nightmare, thanked the judge and prosecutors. "Now that it's been established that a condom can save our life in this time of AIDS," she announced, "in my case and in cases in the future, self-defense does not equal consent."

Consent was also the issue in Manassas, Virginia, when Lorena Bobbitt sliced off her husband's penis. She said he had just forced her to engage in sex; he called it consensual. "I was crying, and I just wanted to get a glass of water," she recounted to an ABC News reporter. "I was drinking the water and the first thing I saw was the knife."

Consent was the dilemma faced by the rule makers at Antioch College when they promulgated their unworkable new dating regulation. As the fall 1993 semester started, Antioch required all students give each other verbal consent for all types of sexual contact, from the first kiss to whatever else develops between partners. No other school in America saddles its students with such specific rules regarding their dating habits.

"What this establishes," explained Antioch spokesman Jim Mann to Associated Press reporter James Hannah, "is 'I did say no.' It also establishes that if someone is drunk or passed out, they do not have the ability to consent. On one level it has been widely supported, on another level it has been greeted with some humor."

The wording of the policy is: "Verbal consent should be obtained with each new level of physical and/or sexual contact or conduct in any given interaction, regardless of who initiates it. Asking, 'Do you want to have sex with me?' is not enough. The request for consent must be specific for each act."

Students who violate the rule can be expelled from the school, although proving a violation stemming from an intimate situation to which only two people are privy seems problematic at best. Perhaps concerned Antioch students will bring tape recorders on their dates as modern electronic escorts.

■

"What do women want?" Freud asked rhetorically after his years of study failed to provide him with an adequate answer. And what do men want? Even the critical classmate of the Glen Ridge rapists, Josh Golin, acknowledges that the wild lifestyle of his peers intrigued him.

Long after he and I chatted, his explanation of the lure of the fast, predatory sex scene at Glen Ridge High haunted me: "They certainly talked a lot more about sex and things they had done. But they had done a lot more things than the people I was hanging out with. When I would hear them talk, I would be like, That's wrong to be talking about girls that you fooled around with. That would be part of me. But part of me would also be like, Wow, they did that and they did that." And then his straightforward confession: "I mean, I don't know what would have happened if me and my friends were, you know, I don't think we would have been like that, but I'm sure in some way we would have, actually."

The question of consent seems like such an easy one to answer. *Yes* means *yes*. *No* means *no*. But communication among people is never so simple. We misunderstand each other. We say one thing and confuse our verbal message with our body language. Sometimes we don't know for sure ourselves if we mean yes or no. We are susceptible to disorienting influences from the contradictory and confounding moral messages of popular culture that batter us day and night, wherever we turn. The new Antioch College policy may seem silly at first blush and even unworkable. But the intent is clear, and it does respond to a real need. We need to know what we want, what our partner or partners want. And we must do all we can to ascertain—in our sex lives and the rest of our lives—that we have truly answered the question of consent.

Select
Bibliography

Against Our Will: Men, Women and Rape (New York: Simon and Schuster, 1975) is Susan Brownmiller's landmark study of rape.

Transforming a Rape Culture is a stimulating collection of essays edited by Emilie Buchwald, Pamela R. Fletcher, and Martha Roth designed to motivate societal change (Minneapolis: Milkweed Editions, 1993).

University of Southern California Law School professor and rape victim Susan Estrich deals specifically with the victimization of raped women in *Real Rape* (Cambridge: Harvard University Press, 1987). She was mightily impressed with the work of the Essex County prosecutors in the Glen Ridge case, telling the *New York Times* during the trial, "The prosecutor here needs to make the argument that 'yes' means 'no,' which is virtually unprecedented."

Robin Warshaw is the author of the Ms. Foundation for Education and Communication report on date and acquaintance rape, *I Never Called It Rape* (New York: Harper & Row, 1988).

University of California, Berkeley, social welfare and social services professor Neil Gilbert challenges *I Never Called It Rape*, and the research by Mary Koss on which it was based, in his article in the

May/June 1992 edition of *Social Science and Modern Society*, "Realities and Mythologies of Rape."

Peggy Reeves Sanday compiled her research on gang rape committed in fraternity houses in *Fraternity Gang Rape: Sex, Brotherhood, and Privilege on Campus* (New York: New York University Press, 1990).

The Beauty Myth, an assessment of, as the subtitle puts it, "How Images of Beauty Are Used Against Women," was written by Naomi Wolf (New York: William Morrow, 1991).

Camille Paglia attacks traditional American feminist analyses of rape—especially acquaintance rape—in her collection of essays *Sex, Art, and American Culture* (New York: Vintage, 1992).

Warren Farrell, past board member of the National Organization for Women, rejects attempts to place all the blame for rape on men in *The Myth of Male Power* (New York: Simon & Schuster, 1993).

Another new voice attacking traditional feminist concerns about acquaintance rape is Katie Roiphe in her school-days memoir, *The Morning After: Sex, Fear and Feminism on Campus* (New York: Little, Brown, 1993).

Books by two New York prosecutors deal with sex offenders and the law. Alice Vachss wrote *Sex Crimes: Ten Years on the Front Lines Prosecuting Rapists and Confronting Their Collaborators* (New York: Random House, 1993), and Linda Fairstein's book is *Sexual Violence: Our War Against Rape* (New York: Morrow, 1993).

Foreign object rape is discussed in Hubert Selby's novel *Last Exit to Brooklyn* (New York: Grove Press, 1965) and by William Faulkner in *Sanctuary* (New York: Random House, 1931).

Lolita, invoked by Michael Querques, is Vladimir Nabokov's classic novel (Olympia Press, 1955).

The story behind Querques's disastrous defense in the so-called Pizza Connection case is told in the book *The Pizza Connection: Lawyers, Money, Drugs, Mafia* by Shana Alexander (New York: Weidenfeld and Nicolson, 1988).

Among Havelock Ellis's encyclopedic writings on sex is *Studies in the Psychology of Sex* (New York: Random House, 1942), in which he pays extensive attention to foreign object masturbation.

The Second Sex (New York: Knopf, 1952) is Simone de Beauvoir's detailed examination of women and her call for equality.

J. David Smith and K. Ray Nelson shed light on the sterilization of retarded women in America with their book *The Sterilization of Carrie Buck* (Far Hills, NJ: New Horizon Press, 1989).

The Senate Judiciary Committee rape report, *The Response to Rape: Detours on the Road to Equal Justice*, which includes a summary of the proposed Violence Against Women Act, was reproduced by the committee in May 1993.

Rape in America: A Report to the Nation is the 1992 compilation of research conducted by the National Victims Center and the Crime Victims Research and Treatment Center at the Medical University of South Carolina. One of the few sources of some statistical data on foreign object rape, it is available from the two institutions involved in the study.

Superior Court of New Jersey Law Division: Essex County Indictment No. 4165; State of New Jersey vs. Christopher Archer, Bryant Grober, Kyle Scherzer, and Kevin Scherzer, defendants, is the transcript of trial proceedings.

Acknowledgments

Shortly after the Iron Curtain rose, I taught a class, under the auspices of Media Alliance and in conjunction with the Freie Universität in Berlin, for American journalism students interested in covering Eastern Europe. One of my star students in Berlin was Todd Diamond, who went on to a develop his career as a reporter based in Washington, D.C. His assistance as my chief researcher for *A Question of Consent* was invaluable. Todd combed through years of newspaper clippings, located hard-to-find primary sources who were needed for interviews, and—aided by his youthful appearance—was able to gather information for this project while on location in Glen Ridge, without drawing inappropriate or counterproductive attention to his activities. His concern with detail and continuing critiques of the work-in-progress were vital and are thoroughly appreciated.

While elements of the population in Glen Ridge responded to the crime by attempting to hide information, the Glen Ridge Free Public Library did just the opposite. My hearty thanks go especially to librarian Ruth Shiels, who worked hard to expeditiously provide me with whatever relevant material she could discover and who clearly values intellectual freedoms.

Malcom Young, the director of The Sentencing Project in Washington, helped me locate needed statistics, as did Dr. Heidi Resnick at the Crime Victims Research and Treatment Center of the Medical University of South Carolina in Charleston.

The Glen Ridge rape case was extensively covered by various news media outlets, and I made frequent reference to the work of my journalist colleagues as I studied and wrote. Particularly valuable were the regular and thorough dispatches filed, as the trial progressed, by Robert Hanley for the *New York Times*.

Several colleagues provided needed assistance, and I specifically want to acknowledge journalist Pat Korten for sharing his Justice Department connections. Dick Rakovan, while general manager of WRC, along with other colleagues at Greater Media, were gracious about making sure I was able to find the time I needed for writing, despite the rigors of our work at the radio station. My agent, Henry Dunow, provided needed guidance, and I thank him. David Mitchell, editor and publisher of the *Point Reyes (California) Light*, helped with some specific research needs.

As usual, the backing of my family is invaluable: my mother, Eva Laufer, my son, Talmage Morris, and my daughter-in-law, Amber Ryan, provided their now-routine, but always needed, enthusiasm and encouragement for the work in progress. My son, Michael Laufer, did an admirable job of trying to keep me cheery during the project. And my wife, Sheila Swan Laufer, offered, as always, continual sustenance and needed advice. The memory of my father was with me as support while I researched and wrote.

I wish to thank my editor, Thomas Christensen, and all the staff at Mercury House, for creating such a constructive and creative workplace. Publisher William Brinton must be singled out for generating the idea to write this book, and I appreciate his confidence.

About the Author

PETER LAUFER is news and program director at WRC radio in Washington, D.C. His previous books from Mercury House are *Nightmare Abroad: Stories of Americans Imprisoned in Foreign Lands* and *Iron Curtain Rising: A Personal Journey through the Changing Landscape of Eastern Europe.*